BRITISH MEDIEVAL CASTLES

BRITISH MEDIEVAL CASTLES

Plantagenet Somerset Fry

DAVID & CHARLES

NEWTON ABBOT LONDON

NORTH POMFRET (VT) VANCOUVER

ISBN 0 7153 6304 2

Set in 12 on 13pt Aldine Bembo
and printed in Great Britain
by Latimer Trend & Company Limited Plymouth
for David & Charles (Holdings) Limited
South Devon House Newton Abbot Devon

Published in the United States of America
by David & Charles Inc North Pomfret
Vermont 05053 USA

Published in Canada
by Douglas David & Charles Limited
3645 McKechnie Drive West Vancouver BC

CONTENTS

LIST OF ILLUSTRATIONS

PLATES

Photographs, unless otherwise stated, provided by the Department of the Environment

IN TEXT

To Fiona, my wife

FOREWORD

In medieval times, there were two principal types of building on the British landscape. One was the cathedral; the other was the castle. Both were extremely important in their own way, for they were not only functional buildings, they were also symbols of the beliefs of their owners. To medieval man they represented strength, permanence and security (of a kind).

No survey of British medieval castles could possibly be undertaken without a study of the many castles saved and kept in good order by the Department of the Environment (formerly the Ministry of Public Building and Works). I have chosen to build this survey by almost exclusive reference to these castles, as they provide a complete history of stone castles in Britain from the eleventh to the sixteenth century. To this Department (and its Scottish Office) I am extremely grateful, not only for material for the text, but also for supplying nearly all the photographs. The patience and helpfulness of the Photographic Library Staff at Hannibal House have been wonderful. I am also very grateful to Peter Woodington for all his line drawings.

Above all, I am deeply indebted to Fiona Whitcombe for her extensive research work and her many suggestions during the preparation of the text, which were invaluable. The book would not have been possible without her help.

Plantagenet Somerset Fry

Chapter 1

'A MAN'S HOUSE IS HIS CASTLE'

The word 'castle' comes from the Latin *castellum*, which meant a fortified dwelling-house. This eventually came to mean the fortified dwelling place of a community, such as a village. A castle in the medieval sense, however, was essentially a structure put up specifically for military purposes, to defend an important geographical position, to house troops and store armaments, and from which to police a district. Far from being a building of romance and chivalry, a castle was a repository of terror and despair. It was the invention and the tool of feudalism. When the need for the castle in England and Wales evaporated in the fourteenth century (castles continued to be needed as military posts in Scotland until the later part of the sixteenth century), it remained the monument to feudalism, a landmark on hill and cliff, in valley and on plain, and it is today an endless source of interest to tourists and trippers.

The first castles were wooden 'motte-and-baileys' introduced into England early in the eleventh century. They were followed by stone castles built by the Normans soon after the Conquest of 1066. These structures were expressly for military use and were never designed for comfort. The attention of the builder was devoted almost entirely to defensive aspects (general shape, wall thicknesses, crenellation, slit windows, etc). There was a progressive improvement in design over the centuries, from the earliest rectangular great towers (or keeps) through polygonal examples, round towers, and the curtain wall with flanking tower types to the concentric castles of the late thirteenth and early fourteenth centuries which represent the climax of military architecture in Britain. These stages were the result of developing siege techniques.

Hardly had the finishing touches been put to the greatest of the concentric castles, in 1330 (Beaumaris), when military tactics began to change and armies started to give up besieging one another in castles. They preferred to fight it out in the open field, as they did, for example, at Crécy in 1346. This change enabled the court and the nobility to acquire more sophisticated tastes in most aspects of living, clothes, food, intellectual pursuits, games, etc. As they were able to pay more attention to standards of comfort in the buildings they lived in, builders were enjoined to think more about environmental aspects when constructing new castles or modifying existing ones.

In 1623, the great English jurist, Sir Edward Coke, in his judgement in the Semayne case made the remark that 'a man's house is his castle'. This has been repeated endlessly ever since, the more familiar version being 'an Englishman's home is his castle'. Coke was emphasising the Englishman's right to defend his home against unlawful entry by the state, in an age when the royal will was often enforced—illegally—by troops of soldiers who billeted themselves in private houses, demanding food, drink and shelter from the owners.

Ironically, by Coke's time the castle had become an anachronism. Although there were several hundred of them dotted about the country, some dating from the reign of William the Conqueror, hardly any were inhabited—or for that matter habitable. They were relics of a bygone feudal era, gaunt, decaying structures of stone dominating the scenery in one or another part of the countryside, as many still do today. There was no living person in England or Wales who remembered—indeed, whose grandfather would have remembered—how castles looked in their medieval heyday, what it was like to live in them, or how they affected the neighbourhood in which they stood.

In the seventeenth century, people had to imagine all these things and that is how the legends about castles began. From then onwards writers and poets fostered the romantic legends of castle life, with lords, knights and their ladies, richly clothed and jewelled, gathered round log fires or seated at raised tables feasting in the great hall, recalling deeds of valour and planning the next day's jousting or hunting.

Castles were not like that at all. By lifting the curtain of history a little we can see that they were dark, forbidding and claustrophobic structures, in which no one stayed for a moment longer than he had to. The twentieth-century visitor who is in anyway susceptible to atmosphere senses this gloom in such castles as Hedingham, Rochester, Richmond and the Tower of London. When these castles had to be occupied by their owners, with their families and retainers, whether in times of siege or in more peaceful days, conditions were appalling. A besieged castle might well be surrendered much earlier than otherwise because living conditions had become so foul. A well-known instance was the surrender of Rochester in 1088 because the odours inside became unbearable.

Lords, knights and men of wealth often preferred to live in halls, or granges, which originated in Anglo-Saxon times and which continued to be constructed in wood or stone or a mixture of the two with little modification right down to the end of the Middle Ages. Most of the building was taken up with a vast room reaching from ground to roof, though soon after the Conquest, these halls were elevated on stilts or arches for security reasons. At one end a small part was usually divided into two storeys, the upper a solar (or bedroom which was also used as a private sitting-room) and the lower a cellar. More rooms could be added to provide kitchen facilities, a chapel, and guest rooms. Sometimes these were separate buildings near the hall, the whole surrounded by a wall.

Since these halls were chiefly residential and not defensive, they were generously endowed with doors and windows, and on the whole were more tolerable places in which to live.

Another house favoured by lords and knights—and particularly by kings—was the unfortified hunting-lodge. Henry II built one, said to be his favourite, at Woodstock on the site of what is now Blenheim Palace. His mistress, Rosamond Clifford, lived here for many years.

While castles were not an essential part of the housing scene, and such accommodation as they did provide was regarded as a second residence, they were very much a part of the landscape. They were sited to control important riverways (Rochester, Goodrich), ports (Orford, Dover), or to police the borders between England and Wales (Chepstow, built by the Normans, Ewloe, Welsh-built) and between England and Scotland (Norham, a Norman castle, and Caerlaverock, a Scottish castle). But these were not the only geographical considerations. They had to be built as near as possible to sources of building materials, such as forests and quarries, or even near Roman ruins, although some wooden castles were built from prefabricated parts shipped from Normandy (see page 27) and the facing for several stone castles brought from Caen where the best ashlar was quarried (see page 43).

Castles were only used by the court as residences when there was nowhere else more comfortable to stay. Medieval kings travelled ceaselessly about their domains, putting down rebellions, presiding over courts of justice, granting charters to towns, or visiting relatives and friends. Like the nobles and the knights, they much preferred the halls and hunting-lodges, and probably used the castles only when there was nothing better in the neighbourhood. Henry II, notorious for his indefatigable travelling—he made his courtiers' lives hell—convened royal councils at Woodstock hunting-lodge and at Clarendon lodge, near Salisbury. Both John and Henry III complained bitterly about the stink and squalor of such and such castles at which they had stayed.

Castles were loathed even more by the ordinary people to whom they represented terror and violence. They were particularly hated by villagers and country people who could be seized and imprisoned without warning or without trial. They did not have the protection that townsfolk enjoyed behind their walls. The terror they endured in Stephen's reign (1135–54) is described in the last pages of the *Anglo-Saxon Chronicle*:

> ... they filled the land with castles. They burdened the unhappy people of the country with forced labour on the castles; and when they were built they filled them with devils and wicked men. By night and day they seized those whom they believed to have any wealth ... and in order to get their gold and silver they put them in prison and tortured them with unspeakable tortures ...

This extract appears under the entry for the year 1137 when there was only a handful of stone castles in the country—the White Tower, Colchester, Pevensey, Richmond, to mention a few, and, still being built, Hedingham. The chronicler's remarks also applied to over 100 wooden castles of the motte-and-bailey type, to be dealt with later in this book (Chapter 2).

FEUDALISM—A MILITARY ORDER OF GOVERNMENT

The stark fortresses which were so prominent a feature of the British landscape were the manifestation of a military order of government and a feudal social system. This system grew out of the business of warfare. It was an arrangement by which a man undertook military service in return for protection or money or landholding. Out of this principle of a bargain or compact between one man and another evolved a complex structure which was distinctly favourable to those nearest the top. It was based on the man who could manage a horse.

The success of the Huns and other Asiatic tribes in their campaigns in Europe from the fifth century onwards was due principally to their invention of the stirrup. This simple device enabled a man to ride very quickly and at the same time keep control of his mount. It is astonishing to reflect that highly civilised people like the Persians, the Greeks and the Romans had not developed this tool. The Asiatics had also learned to breed a type of horse that was faster than any in Europe. These two factors gave them an invincible weapon in war—the mounted soldier who could ride like the wind, manoeuvre at speed and remain securely in the saddle while wielding a sword or a lance, and protecting himself with a shield.

Under Charlemagne, who made the first successful attempt after the collapse of the Roman Empire in the West to unite any sizeable part of western Europe, mounted horsemen had become the lynchpin of the army, for they had adopted the stirrup and had mastered the skills of the cavalryman. But these skills were not acquired overnight. It was a costly business to equip and train men to perform mounted operations effectively, and it limited the number who could become expert cavalrymen. This encouraged the growth of an élite, and eventually gave rise to the concept of chivalry (*chevalerie*). Only people with some wealth, such as large landowners, could afford either to be or to hire cavalrymen. If he was a strong man, such as Charlemagne or Otto the Great, these men served their emperor, or in times of weakness in central government, they fought among themselves for self-aggrandisement. In return for grants of land and certain jurisdictional rights over its occupants they swore oaths to provide emperors or kings with cavalrymen in support of offensive or defensive policies. It is easy to see that as some men acquired more land than others a class structure evolved. Smaller landowners were granted rights by larger landowners in return for service, and so on down to the individual trained cavalryman whose only possession might be a suit of good

Page 17 (*above*) Beaumaris Castle, Anglesey. A very fine concentric castle, built largely by Edward I; (*below*) Carisbrooke Castle, Isle of Wight. A twelfth-century polygonal shell keep on an eleventh-century motte. This is in the north-east corner of the inner curtain

Page 18 (*above*) Restormel Castle, Cornwall. A twelfth-century shell keep on an older motte. Note the earlier gateway by the steep stairway; (*below*) Clifford's Tower, York. A thirteenth-century shell keep of quatrefoil plan on an eleventh-century motte

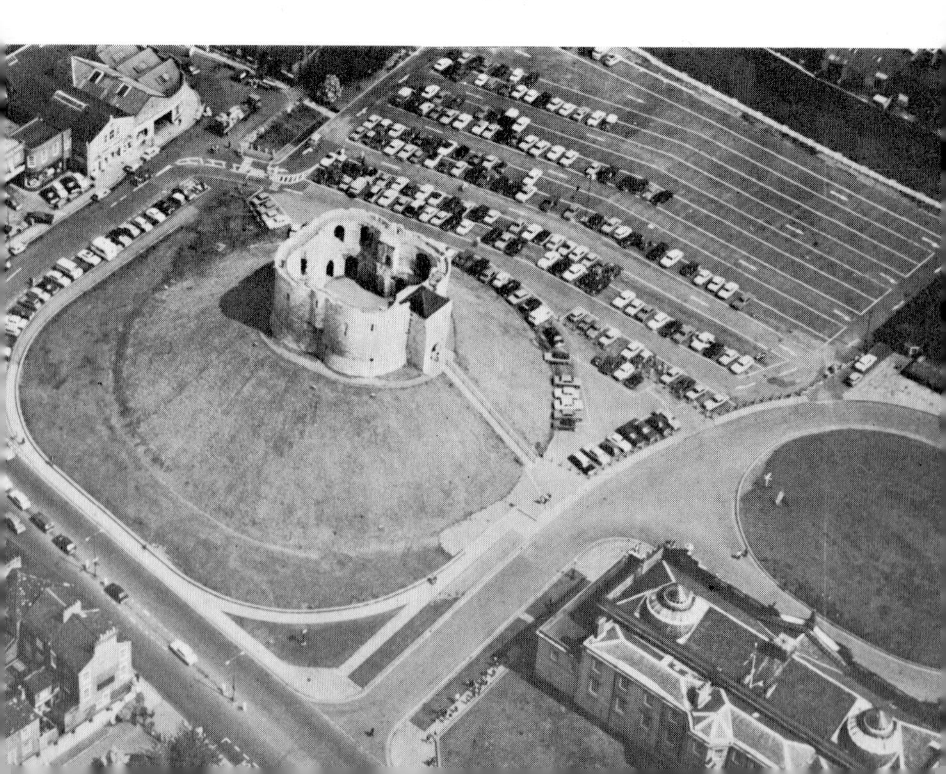

armour, a record of prowess in the field and plenty of guts.

This process is more simply called vassalage which for a long time meant a duty of serving as a cavalryman. Such men were called chevaliers or knights. The reciprocal rights and duties of lords and their vassals took a long time to emerge with any sort of clarity, but by the eleventh century (as Arnold's *A Social History of England* makes clear) it was the lord's duty to come to their vassals' assistance if

> they were attacked by an enemy, to stand by them in a court of law, and to do justice between them in a court of his own in accordance with a body of rules that came to be known as 'feudal custom'. Over and above the obligation to fight on horseback at his lord's side, it was the duty of a military vassal to reverence his lord, to attend his feudal court, to give him the benefit of his advice, to refrain from injuring him by word or by deed, to safeguard his interests in every possible way, and actively to assist him in any enterprise that he might undertake.

Such were the people who spent some part of their lives in castles or behind castle walls.

Vassals were not indissolubly bound to their lords, though there were plenty of kings and lords who tried one way or another to bind them to a long-term contract. A vassal could break his contract if his lord abused his side of it. This underlined a major defect of the whole system, namely, that the sanctity—or effectiveness—of the contract depended to a large extent upon the personalities of the two parties to it. There was no way of enforcing it if one party had—or imagined he had—a grievance against the other. And since the majority of those who were parties to these bargains were men of very limited emotional restraint, whose feelings were more or less permanently on the boil, it required the highest qualities of courage, endurance and fairness, a sound record of military success, plenty of land and money, and much cunning to give a bargain any sort of permanence. Besides Charlemagne and Otto, these qualities reposed in William of Normandy.

William's vassals in Normandy were under obligation to serve him for only forty days in the year and then exclusively in defence of the duchy. His projected invasion of England, therefore, dictated a completely new arrangement which gave him an opportunity to build a feudal structure free of some of the more glaring defects of the European order.

What he did was quite simple. He created a small but extremely effective army of relatives, friends, vassals and retainers, some 6,000 men only, and offered to share out the country with the senior men. When one considers that the area of England is about 50,000 square miles, and that William was planning to give them more than half of it, it was an unparalleled offer. The supreme self-confidence of the man has never ceased to astonish the historian. In offering this land, however, William made it perfectly clear that it was to be held on knight-service, that the volunteers—for that is what they were—would remain tenants-in-chief. William moreover was determined the decision as to who should have what lands in England should be his. His relatives and closest friends were to have the most dangerous areas, which could be invaded, like the south-eastern counties, East Anglia, the Isle of Wight, and the counties on the Welsh and Scottish borders. Those he did not want for himself or for the church (he had to bribe the church to acquiesce in what was to be an act of flagrant aggression) he allotted to about 150 senior relatives and nobles, many of whose names grace the roll of Battle Abbey, some of whom have descendants living.

These Norman adventurers bore no resemblance whatsoever to the medieval conception of chivalrous and courtly knights as portrayed in the works of Chaucer or Sir Thomas Malory. They were only half civilised. Illiterate—and happy to be so—the summit of their ambitions was to have greater power and more land than the next man. Their lives, when they were not fighting or training to fight, were boring and unproductive. Such pretensions that they had to the concept of honour were limited to an insistence upon what they deemed to be their rights, irrespective of the rights of anyone else. Loyalty was outside their comprehension; if they stuck by a superior it was because he could afford to pay for their allegiance.

They indulged in continual private feuding in which the only people who really suffered were the peasantry, who had to put up with endless interruptions of their farming work and whose wooden and thatched shacks were burned down with sickening monotony. As C. T. Wood pointed out in *The Age of Chivalry*, the life of a knight probably had its momentary attractions, 'especially for the knights still in the vigour of youth, but it is difficult to believe that over the years it could have provided many men with much sense of gratification or fulfilment. Indeed, perhaps the saving grace of this life was that few lived long enough to experience its shortcomings.' Even as late as the end of the twelfth century, Usamah, a Moslem contemporary of the great Sultan Saladin, one of the most cultivated rulers ever to emerge in the story of Islam, was describing some Crusader knights as 'animals, possessing the virtues of courage and fighting, but nothing else'.

These close-cropped, unlettered men who came to England found their Anglo-Saxon adversaries much more cultured. The English thegns wore their hair long and some sported beards. Many of them were well educated, familiar with the important literary or historical works of people like Boethius, St Augustine, Alfred the Great and Bede. They dressed elegantly, if the Bayeux Tapestry is not at fault. They were proud of their traditions and their way of life. They treated their women with respect and accorded them a status in their law (women were allowed to hold land). They enjoyed music and poetry, and were inspired to high ideals by the imagery and evocations of their poets. Indeed, they would have been extremely receptive to the ideals of chivalry which were to spread through Europe in the next century.

When the Normans overran England, they confiscated the estates of those Anglo-Saxon nobles who died at Hastings—and also those of many of the survivors, too—and embarked on a policy of apartheid, as it were, by which the remnants of the Anglo-Saxon nobility descended rapidly to the status of simple peasant farmers. Some thegns left England and joined the armies of the Byzantine emperor fighting the Normans in Sicily and Southern Italy, which may have afforded them some sense of revenge.

This hiatus between the Normans and the Anglo-Saxons continued for many years, and it was emphasised in numerous ways. One of the most provocative was the employment of hundreds of them—craftsmen and peasants alike—as builders of the new network of wooden castles designed by the Normans to dominate the people.

Chapter 2

THE MOTTE-AND-BAILEY CASTLE

Before the Norman Conquest a few castles had been built in England and Wales, put up by Norman friends of Edward the Confessor in the years 1042–66. They were chiefly near the border with Wales, at Hereford, Leominster and Richard's Castle, near Ludlow, to mention but three. They were of the wooden motte-and-bailey type, and they were perhaps the first glimpse that the English and Welsh had of continental feudalism at work.

When the Normans conquered England, they set out to keep down the defeated Anglo-Saxons by a calculated policy of terror. One manifestation of this was a programme of building castles up and down the country, some at strategic points commanding roads or rivers or ports, others on high ground which dominated the landscape. Most of these were mottes-and-baileys, though this period also witnessed the beginnings of stone-built castles, such as the White Tower of London, Colchester, Richmond in Yorkshire and Pevensey. 'They built castles far and wide throughout the land, oppressing the unhappy people,' complained the *Anglo-Saxon Chronicle*, 'and things went from bad to worse.'

The motte-and-bailey castle was a simple construction. About fifty were erected between 1066 and 1086 (another estimate is about 100 between 1050 and 1100), each different from the next, but all conforming to one basic plan. Among those mentioned in *Domesday Book* (1086–7) are Berkhamsted, Cainhoe (Beds), Eye (Suffolk), Dudley (Worcs), Laxton,

Dunster (Somerset), Tamworth (Staffs), Belvoir (Rutland), Thetford (Norfolk) and Pontefract. The motte, a high, cone-shaped mound of earth with a flat top, was adapted from a natural hill or rock structure, or artificially raised, the earth being dug out in a circle round the motte to create a V-shaped defensive ditch, deep enough to contain a few feet of mud and water. Its sides were sometimes lined with timber to make them virtually unclimbable. As it was impossible to dig much below the water-line, the larger mottes were not composed entirely of earth taken out of the surrounding ditch. Often, existing earthworks, burial mounds and even buildings were used as the basis for a motte. York Castle was built over a crouched burial mound, and Castle Hill at Thetford, at over 80ft high the tallest motte in Britain, was raised over an Iron Age hill fort. The small motte at Cambridge was put up over a Saxon graveyard, and Oxford motte was on Saxon pits. Materials used for building mottes were sand, loam, stones, chalk or clay, loose or tightly rammed. The two mottes at Lewes were built of roughly squared chalk blocks, while the motte at Oxford (like many others) was coated with clay to prevent the sides from slipping away.

The flat top of a motte was usually surrounded with a palisade of timber planks with sharpened points, generally a foot or two higher than the average height of a man. Occasional slits in the palisade and a wooden watchtower in the middle of the motte allowed the defenders to see out. The larger towers were used as residences as well as look-out posts, although they cannot have been occupied for more than a few days or so at a time.

At the bottom of the motte was the bailey, or courtyard, also circular or elliptical in shape, an enclosure surrounded by a wooden wall, around which another ditch was dug. The bailey contained wooden buildings, such as a house for the owner or for his retainer, stabling for horses, barns for grain, a chapel, and other structures according to the size. The area of

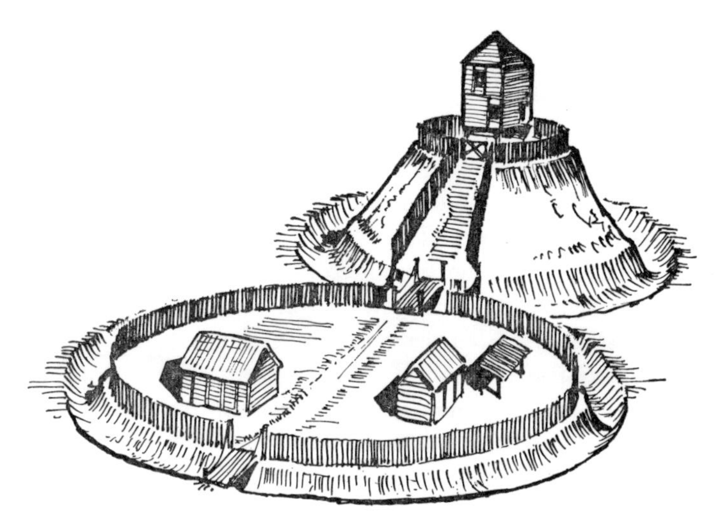

A typical motte-and-bailey

a bailey was anything from 1 to 3 acres on average. Entrance was through one gate only, approached over a drop bridge of timber over the ditch. The motte also had a separate entrance from the bailey, across a bridge over the motte ditch, up a wooden causeway and in through the palisade gate at the top.

It was not easy, therefore, to get into the motte, which was in effect a fortress within a fortress. Both motte and bailey were further protected by a stockade which ran in two directions down from the motte palisade across the motte ditch and joining up with the bailey wall.

Basically, the plan was key-hole shaped, like Trecastle in Brecknockshire, Berkhamsted in Hertfordshire and Pleshey in Essex, but it varied considerably. Sometimes there were double baileys, such as at Ongar in Essex and Windsor in Berkshire, and sometimes, as at Lewes, two mottes. The height of the motte varied, too. Thetford's record 80+ft is nearly equalled at Ongar and Pleshey, while Berkhamsted, at 35ft to

45ft is nearer the average. Most baileys were also several feet higher than the surrounding countryside, though Restormel in Cornwall and Ogmore in Glamorgan are exceptional.

The motte-and-bailey originated, it seems, in France, probably at the beginning of the eleventh century. There is a record of one on the Loire which was similar to those built in Britain. The Bayeux Tapestry depicts the construction of one at Hastings by the Conqueror *before* the battle, and an attack on one already built at Dinan in France.

As a system of defence the motte-and-bailey was effective, though of course it was vulnerable to fire. If the woodwork was draped with wet hides or splashed with buckets of water, not always easily supplied from ditches which did not hold water well, they might survive an attack of arson. But the many references to the burning of castles of the time suggest either that water was short or that fire-fighting methods were not very efficient. The tower on the motte might have a better chance of survival if it was high, for a flaming bolt shot from ground level might reasonably be expected not to reach its target, or since it was travelling at its lowest speed at that height, it could probably be deflected. Similarly, scaling ladders were more hazardous to use against higher mottes and towers.

A simple motte-and-bailey could be erected inside a week, though this depended upon the availability of labour, either voluntary with payment or by conscription. When the Normans had overrun England they were able to press the Anglo-Saxons into service as builders. The first of William's mottes at York (1068) took only eight days. The speed of erection, however, underlines the temporary nature of these mottes. Timber planks hammered down into earth, especially where the earth was a bank of a water-filled ditch, soon rotted away and so required continual inspection and renewal. While this might be acceptable to garrisons occupying mottes in time of war or civil disturbance, it was a different matter if any prolonged residence in peacetime was contemplated.

Of course, Normans and Anglo-Saxons—and Welshmen, too—had long been used to living and going about their business in wooden buildings, like halls and lodges, and they had shrugged off the maintenance problem as part of their way of life, but it cannot have been quite so easy inside the bailey which had to be maintained in a state of constant readiness against attack. These mottes were not intended to be domestic residences. The Conqueror's followers never stopped for long in one place, and were quite used to a nomadic existence moving from one home to another. The mottes were really guard posts by communication centres and were garrison quarters for troops stationed to keep order in restive areas. In other words, they were short-term military camps.

Later mottes may have been more refined in their apartments. Brown records a description of one by a French writer, penned at the end of the twelfth century, which sounds much more like a late medieval mansion.

Since mottes generally had to be put up quickly, nothing was allowed to stand in the way of their erection. Over a hundred houses were knocked down in Norwich to make way for a castle, and Norwich was then the second largest town in England. One-hundred and sixty-six were demolished in Lincoln, and Trevelyan thought that the 478 houses knocked down in Oxford (an undertaking noted in *Domesday Book* and described as 'waste') were probably removed for the castle which went up not long after 1066. These castles were almost always put up using forced labour—a factor which helps to explain the speed of building. Another contribution to fast work was William I's foresight in having timbers for some mottes cut and prepared for assembly in Normandy and shipped to England as prefabricated parts. They were cut to size, pinned and framed, ready for instant construction on site, the bolts and nuts being brought over in barrels along with the main parts.

Mottes were very strong defences against attack by cavalry

and much more so against the footslogging supporters of such Anglo-Saxon rebels as Waltheof, Edwin and Morcar, and Hereward. Their strategic siting meant that their garrisons effectively controlled communications between villages and towns and stopped reinforcements from one reaching the aid of another. The motte at Thetford, though taller than all the others, was typical in many respects. We may look more closely at it.

This huge structure was put up shortly after the Conquest. The motte, over 80ft high and more than 1000ft round the base, must have required a prodigious amount of digging to construct. It stands near the river Ouse in a strategic position overlooking Icknield Way, and surrounding it are the remains of what were massive ramparts—they are huge and forbidding to-day. Walking around the motte which now has a clump of trees on its flat top and many more trees clinging to its sides at angles which seem to defy gravity, one is astonished at its massiveness. Its sides are 45° or more from the horizontal, steeper than the sides of Silbury Hill, near Marlborough.

Looking back some nine hundred years, it is hard to imagine how any army could possibly have besieged the fort on the top. Beneath a top layer of chalk rubble, the mound seems to have been of earth. One morning's rain would have made the sides unscaleable. What was it like in its first weeks before any grass or shrubs or roots had had a chance to grow to cover the mud? Unless you could capture the timber-built causeway from the moat bridge or the fort gate, the only way in was by crawling up the sides yard by yard, hammering wooden stakes into the earth and then using these for ropes for pulling up yourself and your colleagues, one stake at a time—a sitting target for the garrison on top which could pelt you with all manner of missiles or slop liquids over you. An assault of this kind demanded the highest courage and endurance. To be successful it also had to be launched by an army far superior in numbers to that of the defenders, for many would die or be mangled before the top was scaled and a break-in achieved.

This left three ways of forcing a surrender: a protracted siege involving cutting off all supplies to the garrison; an assault with flaming arrows and torches (though these were rendered ineffective by using wet hides or clay-type plaster on the walls); or attack using more sophisticated siege artillery like trebuchets and mangonels, though these were not to reach England until the twelfth century.

Thetford Castle lasted until the reign of Henry II (1154–89) who ordered it to be dismantled.

A trebuchet

Most mottes were put up in towns or on sites of Anglo-Saxon forts. Some, such as Tutbury, were really no more than fortified houses. A castle in a town naturally played a vital part in the town's defence against enemies. And it had another purpose, to dominate—and to be seen to dominate—the town. Often, as at Hereford, Cambridge, Bedford, Shrewsbury, Chester and Stamford, it was sited near a river so that access could more easily be provided for a relieving force or so that the garrison could escape if the town were set on fire.

The widespread construction of mottes was arranged under

strict supervision by the Conqueror or his agents. It was an unruly age and he correctly foresaw that vassals given land and allowed to build castles would be a continual source of danger to the order of the land. So no castles were to be built without his express leave, and privately constructed castles were to be held on the clear understanding that they would be surrendered to him at once on demand. These were brave terms, and it says much for the amazing hold he had over his vassals that few of them rebelled in England in his time. Among those that did were two relatives, his cousin Roger, Earl of Hereford, in 1075, and his half-brother, Odo, Bishop of Bayeux, in 1082.

By 1086 William had distributed the lands of England among his followers and to the Church. He retained about a quarter of the total for himself, and this included much forest land as he loved hunting. A very small amount was left in the hands of a few Anglo-Saxon nobles who had agreed to accept the Norman arrangement.

Following Anglo-Saxon custom, and to preserve some continuity of tenure, the estates the Normans took over from the Anglo-Saxons were scattered far and wide throughout the country. Both sides seem to have appreciated the practice. To William it had the advantage of preventing rebellious nobles from consolidating their strength. The nobles on their part felt that scattered estates gave them the opportunity to extend their influence. In practice it meant that both king and barons were always on the move about their domains. Food could not be stored for long nor could it be easily transported. So, noble households, like the royal court, could never stay in one place for more than a few days—or weeks at the most—time just to eat the flesh, fish, grain and honey in the larders. A fundamental division in medieval society was thus created—between those who stayed in one place tilling the earth and bound to it as serfs, and their unproductive masters, perpetually travelling the dreadful medieval roads in huge caravans, or riding and fighting their way from manor to manor, castle to castle.

The Conqueror died in 1087. A year earlier he had given a splendid demonstration of his power at Salisbury by demanding—and getting—an oath of fealty from 'all the landowners who were of any account throughout England, no matter whose vassals they might be. All did him homage and became his men' (*Anglo-Saxon Chronicle*, 1086). It was the apex of a remarkable man's reign.

The business of castle building went on unabated in the reigns of his two sons, William II (Rufus) and Henry I. O'Neil estimates that there were about 100 castles in England and in the Marches of Wales by 1100, though other historians have put the figure as high as 500. Some, incidentally, were erected in the Isle of Man, which at this time belonged to Norway.

In 1120, Henry's son and heir, William, was drowned at sea and this left his daughter, Matilda, as heir presumptive. The barons were not likely to accept a woman as ruler, but because the king regarded their preferred candidate, his nephew Stephen, Count of Blois, a grandson of the Conqueror, as weak and unfitted to succeed, he compelled them to swear an oath to recognise Matilda who was then the wife of Geoffrey Plantagenet, Count of Anjou.

As soon as Henry was dead, the chaos he feared broke out. Turning a blind eye to their oath, and knowing Stephen for what he was, the nobles offered him the throne. Despite his promise to Henry that he, too, would support Matilda, he accepted, and the nobles reverted with delight to their old pastime of feuding. For nineteen years England endured the cruelties and indignities so aptly described by the *Anglo-Saxon Chronicle*, the extract from which is quoted on page 15. These 'terrible traitors', as the chronicler called them, threw up scores of new mottes all over England. These are referred to as adulterine castles because they were not licensed by the king. Indeed, many were put up in flat defiance of his will. These mottes proved very effective. The garrisons had only to dominate a few square miles of farmland below to be able to hold out for prolonged periods of time.

At Ludlow, which had a stone wall and gatehouse, the garrison resisted a siege by the king. One morning, he and Prince Henry of Scotland were walking round the base of the tower when a grappling iron on the end of a rope was suddenly thrown down, its hook catching the prince's cloak. Gradually the prince was lifted off the ground up the wall. With considerable presence of mind Stephen grabbed at the prince's feet and held fast while the victim pulled out a knife and slashed at the rope.

This is an interesting incident, as it shows how closely involved in warfare medieval rulers often were in those times. James II of Scotland (1437–60) was killed directing an artillery barrage in the siege of Roxburgh Castle, when a cannon exploded near him. Cardinal Richelieu of France personally conducted the siege of La Rochelle in 1627.

In 1154, Stephen died and was succeeded by Henry II, Matilda's son, and the first of the Plantagenet dynasty. This great ruler at once set about restoring order in the country, and one of the first acts was to order the demolition of all the adulterine castles. It is said that some 350 received his attention.

Although a few stone towers and walls had been built before 1154, it was Henry who embarked on the first major programme of stone castle construction in England. His motives were both military and administrative. He kept tight control of the programme. Some of the castles were superimposed upon earlier mottes, such as at Windsor, Arundel, Carisbrooke, Cardiff, Totnes and Warkworth. But the new programme took a long time, for these stone structures were not put up in a matter of weeks or even months. As a result new styles of architecture were being tried out before older ones had been abandoned, as will be clear in the next chapter.

Chapter 3

THE FIRST CASTLES IN STONE

While some castles had been built of stone before the coming of Henry II, they were few and far between, and we do not know which of them was the first. One which has a good claim—and which now attracts more tourists than any other ancient building in the United Kingdom—is the White Tower, started by William the Conqueror. This splendid building is so named because in the Middle Ages it was often given a coat of whitewash on its outside walls. It is an excellent example of a Norman rectangular great tower, though it was the subject of extensive alterations in later years (see page 105).

Mottes had more than proved their effectiveness in many cases, but they could never be of permanent value. The maintenance problem was a constant source of worry. As siege weaponry improved they became less easy to hold against attack. They were not as a rule imposing, unless they were like Thetford, and then only because they were very tall. The Normans appreciated that a structure of stone conveyed much better the impression of dominion they wanted to create in England. Nor were mottes pleasant or architecturally aesthetic, and the Normans liked beautiful things.

As most of the mottes had been erected in positions of strategic importance, so the Normans built their stone castles in like positions. If the sites were flat, an artificial mound would be thrown up, but the builders preferred natural rising ground or rocky outcrops overlooking river valleys or the sea. There, they built two main types of castle to begin with, the shell keep and the rectangular (or square) great tower.

The shell keep was a natural development of the earth and wood motte. It was generally an enclosure of stone walling in circular, polygonal or quatrefoil shape. The enclosing wall was called the curtain, a term later used for the walling in inner and outer baileys. The interior of the shell contained buildings of one kind or another—dining hall, chapel, troops' quarters, stores, guests' rooms, lodgings for servants—and they were erected against the inside of the curtain, whether made of stone or of wood. The stonework of the curtain which acted as the outside wall to all buildings, was about 10 to 12ft thick and it sat on foundations sunk 6 or 7ft into tightly packed earth. The curtain heights varied considerably, anything from 15 to 30ft. Occasionally, a stone curtain was put up on the exact line of the palisade round an earlier bailey.

Shell keeps were not built quickly. Traces of rooms or buildings added long after the original castle was constructed can be found in many of them. Their development was not at all rapid, indeed, there was really not much difference between a twelfth- and a fourteenth-century shell in the matter of overall design. Many of Edward III's castles were shell keeps. Two excellent examples of early shell keeps which are different from one another are Restormel in Cornwall (page 113) and Carisbrooke in the Isle of Wight (page 134). Restormel is almost completely round, with a gatehouse, on a mound surrounded by a ditch. Carisbrooke is a polygonal shell keep on a mound in one corner of a much larger square-plan bailey with a stone curtain. Clifford's Tower in York (page 18) is an interesting example of a shell of quatrefoil shape. Other shell keeps were at Windsor, Cardiff, Totnes and Trematon.

When building the shell, the designers paid special attention to the gates. Where a castle was of motte-and-bailey layout with stone walls for both motte and bailey, there would be

Page 35 (*right*) Castle Rising, Norfolk. A twelfth-century rectangular great tower with a forebuilding which is of the same height

(*left*) Hedingham Castle, Essex. An early twelfth-century rectangular great tower. Note the shallow buttresses, scaffold holes, and a 45° groove over the doorway which indicates the line of the roof to a fore-building since disappeared

Page 36 (*above*) Richmond Castle, Yorkshire. The eleventh- to twelfth-century rectangular great tower is at the north-east apex of the triangular curtain. The ruins of Scollands Hall are on the left; (*below*) Portchester Castle, Hampshire. A Norman rectangular great tower sited in the north-west corner of a Roman walled quadrangle. The buildings adjacent to the tower are of similar or later date

an upper gate-tower in the motte wall, projecting above it, and another projecting as much as half the curtain height again at the bottom of the stone causeway leading from the upper gate to the bailey curtain. On the other hand, when the castle was a shell on a mound, like Restormel, there was only one gate. In both types, gates had drawbridges to provide platforms over the ditches. A particularly good example of a shell keep was at Arundel, an imposing castle which began as a fort in Anglo-Saxon times. It underwent a long succession of alterations and developments right up to 1643 when in the Civil War it was besieged and severely damaged by Sir William Waller. For a long time it was neglected, but towards the end of the eighteenth century the tenth Duke of Norfolk restored it. In early Norman days it has been a large motte-and-bailey, the motte being about 70ft high and about 600ft round the base. Stonework was superimposed on the earthwork in Henry II's time and the shell wall was about 20ft high and 10ft thick. Henry rather liked the site and he had a garden prepared there in front of his private quarters.

Another interesting shell keep is at Windsor, which has been greatly restored. It is now but a small part of a large complex of castle buildings, towers and walls.

The other type of castle was the great tower surrounded by a wall, with, sometimes, other less important buildings inside the wall. These towers, or keeps as they came to be called as late as the sixteenth century, were either rectangular or square in plan in the earlier years. Later on, they were polygonal, or cylindrical. Most of the towers were sunk so low into the ground that the bottom floor was a basement and you could only get in by a doorway at first-floor level. As they were the last refuge of the besieged inside the bailey in time of war, they had to be as impregnable as possible. They had to be equipped with what went then for comforts and conveniences, though by our standards these would have been unbearable. And they had to be built to last. So they were given very thick walls (those at Dover, for example, are over 20ft in parts) and these were partly solid and partly hollow. In the hollow sections were put the services, staircases, drainage, waterpiping, small rooms, stockrooms, prison cells and so forth. As it turned out, most of these great towers outlasted their usefulness by centuries.

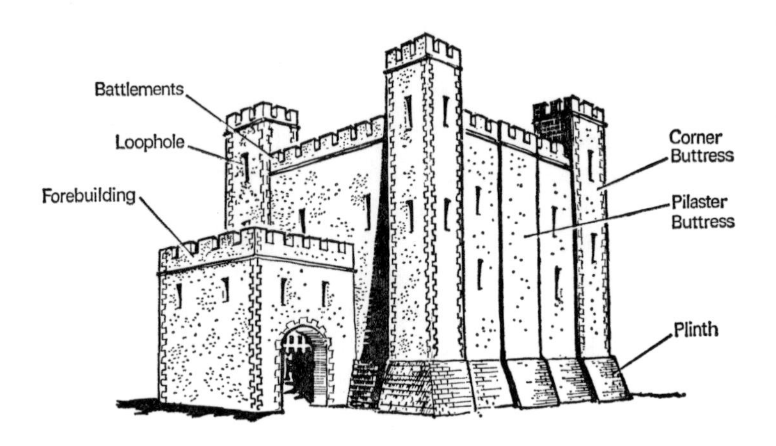

A rectangular great tower

In general, they followed a standard plan, but each one of course differed from the next in many particulars. The towers were usually taller than they were broad, though some of the more oblong ones were slightly less tall than their breadth (Castle Rising, Norwich and Colchester, for example). They had two or three—or in a few instances four—storeys, and a basement. These storeys were sometimes divided by a partition or crosswall, which was not always in the centre. The crosswall enabled defenders to carry on the fight if, as happened at Rochester in 1215, they were driven back from the entrance. Crosswalls also reduced the length of the wooden beams which supported the flooring. A storey might be 35ft or more across in internal measurement. Beams of wood of this length or greater could be cut, but without the availability of steam saws or any other mechanical equipment, the cutting process would take a lot of time. Trees of this length, moreover, were in less plentiful supply than those of, say, about 20ft. The positioning of a crosswall, therefore, whether as solid wall or as an arch or as a row of arches, meant that beams of about 20ft were long enough.

The exteriors of great towers were usually plain and simple in their architecture, though Castle Rising (page 35) and Norwich, among others, were ornamented. Rising usually from a splayed plinth for strength—a feature which provided an excellent bouncing area for missiles and liquids thrown down from the battlements at the top—the flat walls incorporated shallow buttresses which, positioned at the four angles and, sometimes, in the middle of each wall, merged into the plinth. This can often be seen as a feature of ecclesiastical buildings of the same period. Since the tower was principally a fortified refuge, there were few windows and these were invariably very small. Their ornament outside was generally restrained, though Hedingham windows have chevron moulding. Lower down the walls these windows were little more than slits. The windows let in cold and light, but they gave archers little protection. The slits (called loopholes) were equally useless to archers as they could not see the ground from them.

These windows and loopholes made the inside of a great tower dark and gloomy even on a bright day, and unless one was actually sitting or standing by a window it was almost perpetual twilight indoors. To overcome this the walls were often whitewashed to reflect what light did get in but with all the open cooking and the burning of logs and coal to get some heat into the building (an almost superhuman job in itself), whitewash very soon turned to the dirty yellow or grey we associate today with buildings in industrial areas.

Richmond great tower has a roof which has been partly glazed in recent years, but unless the sun is out and overhead, it is very dark inside, as there are hardly any windows or loopholes in the walls.

The top of the tower had a turret at each corner, joined by the battlements, and a parapet outer wall behind which was a walkway. These parapets and turrets were crenellated, that is, provided with openings through which archers could shoot. Crenellation, an essential feature of a tower top—and for a curtain wall in most cases—was only allowed by licence from the king.

A corner turret of a rectangular great tower

The entrance to the great tower was on the first floor, or even higher up in some instances. A portcullis might be fitted in the doorway but this seems to have been the exception. The entrance was usually reached by a stone staircase and this was covered by a stone structure abutting the wall of the tower, and called the forebuilding. This might have its own defences, such as a small turret or some crenellation. In fact the forebuilding was almost a tower in its own right, and in some castles it was quite elaborate, as at Castle Rising and Dover. At the former, moreover, it was about the same height as the great tower, whereas the average height of a forebuilding is about two-thirds of the tower height.

Inside the great tower there were three or four floors and a basement, though at Kenilworth there are only two floors. Working upwards, the basement was lit by loopholes in the wall masonry, so that few activities could be carried out without the aid of torches. Sometimes the basement ceiling was vaulted, and the business area would consist of two main central rooms with smaller chambers and vaults opening off, built within the thickness of the wall or within the forebuilding. Basements were used for storage, and the well supplying the water for the tower generally came up at this level in or near the wall. The shaft was sunk deep into the earth—at Dover it went down to about 350ft. The selection of the site for the tower in the first place will have been dictated to a large extent by the availability of water. The well provided fresh water, but in times of siege there was always the danger of objects being dropped into it. It was also possible to poison the whole garrison of a tower during siege if a spy or traitor got in and contaminated the water, as happened once at Pembroke (see page 136).

The first floor was the entrance floor. In a tall tower like Hedingham, it had a number of small chambers with a variety of uses. While it is believed by some authorities that few great towers had special kitchens as food was cooked in private rooms, there must have been many occasions when food was prepared and cooked on this floor. Another chamber would probably be a chapel, though some chapels are found above the staircase in the forebuilding. Another chamber would be the garderobe, or latrine—no modern water closet but a simple hole in the floor which connected with a drain-shaft built in the wall thickness and leading to the moat or ditch outside or into the foundations. It is not hard to imagine the offensiveness of these garderobes, especially in times of siege when the tower would be occupied by more than twice the usual number of people. In an age which put up with discomforts unthinkable to most of us today, there are several records of complaints about malodorous garderobes. The old motte at Rochester surrendered in 1088 because of the intolerable smells resulting from a period of confinement for many people inside its walls. Henry III complained about the noisomeness at the Tower of London and at Marlborough. Today, these garderobes are often taken for prison cells—quite wrongly.

Access from one floor to the next was usually by spiral staircase, though at Bamborough and Richmond, among others, there were straight flights. The arrangement of the staircases was sometimes alternate, that is, the case from the basement to the first floor was on one side while that from the first to the second was on the opposite side, and so on upwards. This meant that invading troops had to cross the whole floor area to get up the stairs from one floor to the next, thereby running the gauntlet of snipers behind chamber doors or from the gallery in the great hall. Most towers, however, had a continual spiral staircase from basement to roof.

The second floor, usually called the great hall, was high and in many castles, like Hedingham, Richmond, Dover, to mention three, two storeys tall. Halfway up the double height there was a gallery, with iron or wooden balustrades, and additional rooms off into the walls. The name of the great hall, known at Hedingham as the banqueting hall, suggests its principal use. Here the lord and his wife would entertain king, court, friends, and foreign visitors. There might be a dividing crosswall with separate quarters for the lord behind it, called the solar. Otherwise, the lord and his family lived on the floor above. Larger rooms were sometimes divided by wooden partitions with tapestries draped on them or by heavy curtaining. Either way there was little privacy.

Great towers were essentially twelfth-century buildings, with a few exceptions, such as the White Tower. Among the earliest survivors are Goodrich, Hedingham, Rochester and Richmond.

When choosing a site for the great tower and its bailey, the builders took many factors into account, apart from the strategic importance and the proximity to water. Where was the nearest quarry? How much would it cost to use it, if it belonged to the Church? Would any stone have to be quarried on site? Was there any rock on site? Were there any Roman remains nearby? Where was the nearest waterway for transport, as water cartage was cheaper than land cartage? What would it cost to dress the tower in the finest ashlar obtainable, namely, that from Caen in Normandy? Where would the building labourers be found? Where was the nearest timber supply? What was the closest supply of lead? Was there any old rubble from Saxon times available for hard core and infilling?

Questions like these would today be resolved by one or other of the building team of architect, quantity surveyor, consulting engineer, services engineer or contractor, but in the twelfth century no such team existed. Even the stone-masons were not always trained. Everyone took a hand in building in those days. On the lower level it was a very good way to earn money.

Once some, if not all, of these questions were resolved, work began. If there was a rock foundation, the rock was flattened and the plinth of the tower laid down. This was followed by the walls and their buttresses, working upwards using wooden pole scaffolding (you can still see the holes where these scaffolds were inserted into the walls in most surviving great towers, especially at Hedingham). The walls were built not usually of stone alone but of an aggregate of rubble, flintstone, old brick and building rag, held together with a mortar of sand and lime which set the whole as hard as rock. The corners, window lintels, arches and other key parts were of ashlar. If there was no rock foundation, artificial foundations were made by filling trenches somewhat wider than the proposed walls and plinth with an assortment of rubble, stone and timber rammed down hard. The building materials were moved on the site by sledge, two-man stretcher or crude wheelbarrow. They were hauled up the scaffolding in baskets with ropes and pulley wheels. Normally, building work would be suspended in the winter months, but if completion was wanted more quickly it could be continued throughout the year, even by torchlight at night-time.

When the walls were completed they might be coated with plaster or whitewash, and lines imitating joints cut into the plasterwork. How long the whitewash remained clean is not known but it was probably discoloured by smoke and effluent almost as quickly as the walls were inside.

It is not easy to say how long these great towers took to build. There are few satisfactory records. Orford in Suffolk, a newer and more interesting type of tower (see page 114) took eight years, from 1165 to 1173, but this could have included the bailey wall and the other buildings inside it. Renn estimates that it took an average of a year to complete 10ft of wall in a standard castle, but this seems a long time, unless he incorporates the factor that perhaps six months went by with hardly any work being done at all.

Once built, they were, to begin with, all but impregnable, and surrender was only obtained by starving the garrison and the other occupants through cutting off supplies or by poisoning the water. But blockading posed many problems for the besiegers, who had first to encamp outside the curtain possibly for weeks on end. There, temporary buildings of wood or canvas were the only shelter, and these were very vulnerable. Once the curtain had been breached or the gate forced, fighting continued inside, building by building, until the defenders withdrew inside the great tower, when a fresh period of siege would have to be initiated. These towers generally withstood siege artillery, though if the besiegers were lucky enough to get flaming bolts through the narrow windows or rotting animal carcases over the top of the battlements down into the top storey by smashing the roofing timbers and tiles, they might bring surrender earlier than by simpler blockading.

The most effective way to get into a rectangular great tower was by mining and this was done on several occasions, so much so that the technique provoked a series of modifications in castle design which are described in Chapter 4.

MEDIEVAL SIEGE ARTILLERY

When the crusading knights of western Europe went out to the Levant to rescue the Holy Land from those whom they were pleased to call infidels, they had little idea of modern siege techniques. Their activities in this direction had been confined to using fire, to frontal shock assault or to blockade. When they reached the warmer climate of the East they discovered many things. One of these was that the Saracens whom they wanted to dislodge from Palestine were greatly superior to them in almost every facet of civilisation, and this included generations of experience in siegework. They and their principal adversaries, the Byzantines, had been using a whole range of artillery and weaponry almost unknown in the West.

The siege of a fortress followed a routine procedure. First, you softened up the resistance of the defenders by discharging over the battlements of the curtain an assortment of missiles, using a variety of machines known collectively as petraria. One was an arbalest, a very large crossbow which fired metal darts or stones with great accuracy. Another was a mangonel which has a wooden arm pivoted in the centre on a vertical frame, with a spoon at one end and a rope torsion-operated mechanism at the other. A third was a trebuchet, virtually a mechanical sling operated by a counterweight at one end of the arm (page 29). The trebuchet was a development of the mangonel. Both fired a variety of missiles, stones, putrefying animal carcases, and the deadly Greek Fire. This was a chemical liquid, based on naphtha, that resembled napalm in its effects. It was invented by the Egyptian chemist, Callinicus, in about AD 650, who was, fortunately for western Europe, working for the Byzantines. It is said that their monopoly of Greek Fire enabled the Byzantines to withstand everything sent against them by Muslims, Bulgars, pirates alike, for nearly 200 years.

While this barrage was going on, troops of attackers manoeuvred a penthouse, a high tunnel-like structure made of timber and hides, and occasionally with metal plates, close to the walls, and under its protective covering they filled in a stretch of the surrounding moat or ditch. Then they drove a battering ram against the wall to effect a breach. The penthouse was subjected to heavy bombardment by the defenders on the battlements using large stones, hot liquids, ironwork, and fire balls, and as a protective cover it cannot have lasted very long. The attention of the defenders involved in this procedure was often drawn away from the penthouse by other besiegers moving up behind mantlets, that is, moveable sloping screens on wheels, which provided cover for archers who would pick off anyone incautious enough to show himself.

If this was not achieving the desired results, further techniques were employed. The walls were stormed by men carrying scaling ladders. This demanded great courage, for the ladders could easily be deflected from the wall by a simple pole with a Y-shaped end pushed smartly against the top rung. In this kind of assault, sheer weight of numbers played

A mantlet

a decisive part. Another machine also helped and this was a belfry. This was a huge, square-section, portable tower, sometimes on wheels, on the top of which was a platform with a sloping vizor behind which archers could rake the battlements of the castle with close-range fire.

All these techniques were extremely dangerous and the injury and loss of life must have been considerable in every siege.

There were several ways to defeat these weapons. In the long term, curtain walls were built higher and higher. In the shorter term, defenders erected special wooden structures on the wall tops projecting outwards like galleries. These were covered with hides and planks and were called hoardings. They had slatted floors through which defenders dropped stones or liquids on to the attackers. If they were employed on great towers, the splayed plinth at the base with the bouncing qualities came into its own. The flooring was supported by put-logs, that is, square-section beams inserted in square holes in the wall masonry, and these holes can be seen in many surviving castle walls to-day. Occasionally, two

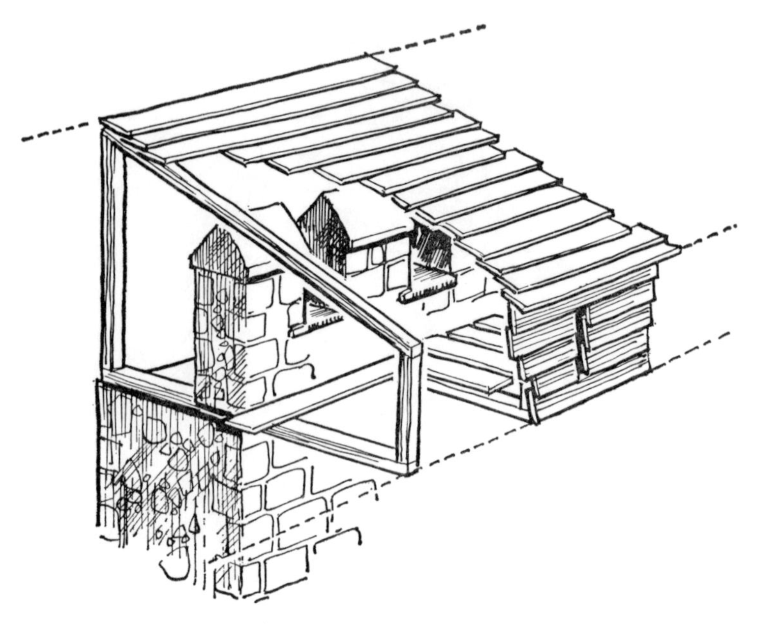

A cut-away section of hoarding

hoardings, one above the other, might be used. But they had their drawbacks. They were made of wood and so did not last. None has survived and so one can only guess at what they looked like. If they were struck by a missle containing Greek Fire they would catch alight at once. A heavy stone could smash a hole in them, breaking the continuity of the structure and exposing the occupants to direct enfilade by the besiegers' archers. These defects were not remedied until stonework machicolations were introduced in towers and curtain walls in the thirteenth century. Machicolation is the word given to the gaps in the hoarding floor. When the parapets were fortified with a permanent stone hoarding, as it were, and given gaps in the stonework for the same purposes, they were called machicolated parapets. A good example surviving is at Raglan Castle in Monmouthshire (page 118).

The Crusaders brought home these siege techniques and used them where they could. But the great towers did not yield to them. The towers were thus subjected more to mining procedures which were directed at the corners. This led to the development of towers without sharp corners. At the same time more attention was paid to the curtain itself which was reinforced with flanking towers. Eventually, great towers were no longer considered essential, for all the apartments they offered could be better provided in separate buildings inside the bailey once the curtain had itself been properly fortified, or an extra curtain added outside and around it. These were to be the developments in castle building in the later twelfth and thirteenth centuries. But great towers were not given up altogether. One of the greatest in Britain is at Bothwell in Lanarkshire, built towards the end of the thirteenth century.

Chapter 4

TWO CENTURIES OF IMPROVEMENTS

NEW SHAPES

The vulnerability of rectangular great towers to mining was amply demonstrated at the siege of Rochester Castle in 1215 by King John in the civil war which followed his assent to *Magna Carta.* Having conducted a barrage of mangonel and trebuchet fire at the curtain for several days, John eventually breached it in the south-eastern area and broke into the bailey. The defenders fought a running battle up to the forebuilding of the great tower and then retired inside. So the king decided to undermine one of the tower corners, and for this purpose he ordered, in a writ of 14 October sent to the sheriffs of Canterbury, urgent supplies of picks for the sappers. A tunnel was dug underneath the south-eastern angle, and wooden planks supported by posts were put up inside it.

Then, according to the *Official Guide to Rochester Castle*, the king ordered his justiciar, Hubert de Burgh, to find 'forty of the fattest pigs of the sort least good for eating to bring fire beneath the tower'. These were to be killed and burned to ensure that the wooden props would catch fire and stay alight even in the airlessness of the tunnel under the corner of the tower. In due course the mine did collapse and, with a fearful rending sound, the corner of the tower burst away from the remainder of the structure, revealing a gaping hole through with the king sent his troops. Inside, the defenders continued to fight behind the crosswall. The tower was not easily overcome even then. Acute shortage of food brought about the desired surrender, in the end. There is, to this day, a reminder of this successful mining operation; the demolished corner of the tower was replaced by a rounded tower corner (see plate on page 107).

There were several answers to mining. Towers built on rock were of course unapproachable. A wide and deep moat round a tower made tunnelling impossible. Another obstacle could be made by filling in the basement of the tower to make it solid. At Kenilworth, for example, each corner had its own solid buttress which would probably not have given way on a collapsed mine. A countermine was also effective. Here, the defenders, having detected or made a reasonable guess at the direction in which the enemy sappers were tunnelling, bored down through the basement floor in the opposite direction. If this was successful, the result was a 'desperate, cramped, hand-to-hand encounter in a dark and choking underground cavity'. The answer really lay, however, in better design, and the next two centuries witnessed a variety of experiments.

In the second half of the twelfth century some new designs were tried out, based largely on examples seen in the Levant and the Byzantine empire. Among the new castles were cylindrical great towers like Pembroke, polygonal towers (Orford, Tickhill and Odiham), cylindrical towers with projecting buttresses (Conisbrough), and curtains with small flanking towers at intervals along the whole length, and containing no great towers (Framlingham, Corfe). In the thirteenth century the concentric castle made its first appearance in Britain. This had two or three rings of curtains interspersed with cylindrical, square or polygonal towers (Beaumaris, Caerphilly, which were new, and London and Dover which were improvements).

The employment of curved surfaces on towers was an obvious answer to mining. It eliminated the angles and so greatly reduced the danger of collapse on to a mine. Cylindrical towers cost less to build, but as the masonry was of uniform strength they were better able to withstand assault. By enclosing the upper part with vaulting, the risk of fire from burning missiles aimed at the roof was minimised. These cylindrical towers did not come suddenly upon the castle scene. There was a transitional stage from the rectangular to the round, and this is illustrated well by considering three castles in sequence, Orford (c.1165–73), Tickhill (c.1179–82) and Conisbrough (c.1185–90).

Orford was said to have been given special attention by Henry II, who had it built to guard the port at Orford on the Suffolk coast and to balance the power of one of his greater barons, Hugh Bigod, Earl of Norfolk. It was designed to a then novel plan, a cylindrical interior with a polygonal exterior of twenty-one sides. Jutting out from the exterior were three buttresses which were thickwalled but with hollow turrets, spaced out equally 120° apart (see page 114). Three crenellated square turret tops enabled the defenders to cover all approaches to the tower.

First-floor plan of Orford great tower

Page 53 (*above*) Pembroke Castle, Wales. The cylindrical great tower of Pembroke Castle was over 70ft high, and its walls were 15ft thick in places; (*below*) Orford Castle, Suffolk. A late twelfth-century polygonal great tower, with twenty-one faces externally with three buttresses. The staircase is in the southern buttress behind the forebuilding

Page 54 (*above*) Conisbrough Castle, Yorkshire. An aerial view of the twelfth-century cylindrical great tower. Note the pronounced splayed plinth at the base and the six buttresses; (*below*) Framlingham, Suffolk. A curtain-wall castle with rectangular flanking towers built at the end of the twelfth century. This was one of the first of this type

Conisbrough in Yorkshire (see page 122), considered by many experts to be one of the best monuments of medieval England, was even more experimental. Built by Hamelin Plantagenet, bastard brother of Henry II, it is cylindrical with six equidistantly space semi-hexagonal buttresses which are almost towers in themselves and which rise out of the splayed plinth of the cylinder. These towers were nearly 100ft high, 20ft deep at the base and 15ft deep at first-floor level. Ashdown reckoned that even if one or two of the buttresses were blown up the stability of the remainder would be affected but little. The tower's entrance is on the first floor and is reached by a flight of steps. This could be covered from a multitude of angles in the two turret tops on either side of the door, so obviating the need for a protective forebuilding.

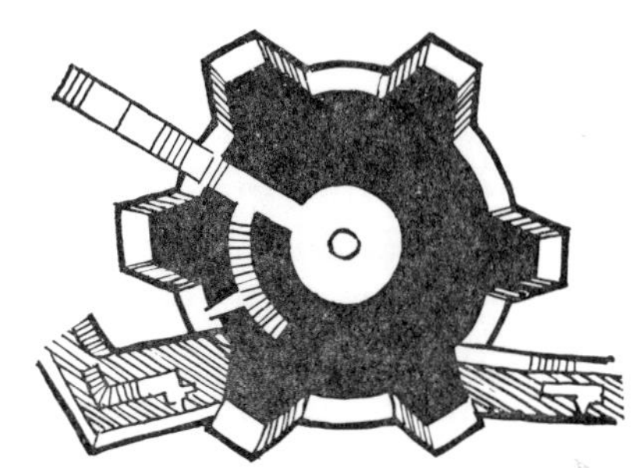

Ground plan of Conisbrough Castle's great tower

Pembroke great tower, one of the first completely cylindrical towers in Britain, was built in about 1200 by William the Marshal, Earl of Pembroke. It sits inside a bailey of nearly 4 acres enclosed by a curtain interspersed with smaller round towers. It was a base for English expeditions to Ireland. The tower is over 70ft high. It has no buttresses, but its base walls are 20ft thick and were sufficiently robust to withstand anything, including a fierce siege by Owain Glyndŵr at the start of the fifteenth century. In its long history it never fell, and when it surrendered in the Civil War it was because the water supply had been poisoned by the Parliamentarians.

The early part of the thirteenth century saw the construction of several cylindrical towers in England and Wales, including Launceston in Cornwall, Longtown in Herefordshire, Dolbadarn in Caernarvonshire (built by the Welsh, not their Anglo-Norman conquerors), and Tretower in Brecknockshire. Later in the century the cylinder designs reached Scotland, the most famous being that at Bothwell, in Lanarkshire.

Cylindrical towers were proved defensively better than rectangular towers but they were environmentally more unsuitable. They were particularly claustrophobic and uncomfortable; they were difficult to furnish, in an age when no one thought further than a rectangular chest, bench or stool; and they were irritatingly uniform. In the earlier years of the cylinder tower experiments were made with square towers with D-ends, such as at Helmsley in Yorkshire, but the idea was not pursued. Like the rectangular tower, the cylindrical towers was perpetually dark, cold and gloomy. The whole place smelt. The building was impossible to heat. If you lit a fire you got a room full of smoke. Unless you cooked in your own quarters your food was cold and probably inedible by the time it was brought up to you. Adding to the discomfort was the noise: boots on the stone stairs or tramping backwards and forwards across the wooden floors, trestles and benches being moved, dogs barking, children yelling, everyone chattering incessantly in an age when very few people could read or write and so expressed themselves vocally. If there were prisoners in the ground-floor chambers or in oubliettes, dungeons entered only through openings in the floor and where, generally forgotten or ignored, captives were left to die, their cries and groans added to the cacophony. This was in peacetime. How much worse it must have been in time of siege when a battery of mangonels and trebuchets kept up a barrage of missiles outside, the enemy troops shouting and roaring the while, the din perhaps drowning the sound of sappers trying to bring part of the wall down.

Hygiene as we know it was unheard of. At Dover, water from the well was piped into all parts of the tower, but what happened under siege as in 1215, when more people packed themselves into the tower and used the primitive sanitary arrangements? Were the garderobes ever cleaned?

Perhaps the most frightening aspect of castle life was the claustrophobia. One has only to walk round the Norman great tower at Hedingham or the Plantagenet Orford to sense the awful feeling of being cooped up, of life closing in on one. At least in peacetime one could go out for a walk inside the bailey ground, but in siegetime you were confined and there was no escape. An assault might take weeks. Food might run out. You might have to resort to eating horseflesh (as the defenders of Rochester did in 1215). The overcrowding would become maddening. People of those times were emotionally extremely volatile, and would lose their tempers at the drop of a hat. The dignity and 'stiff upper lip' attitude now so inextricably associated with the British character just did not exist then. Often the demand for surrender from the besiegers would come to the occupants as a blessed relief.

In time, lords began to move out of great towers and into more commodious and comfortable buildings inside the bailey. But these were unsafe and too exposed in time of siege, when the bailey defences were inadequate. So the military engineers developed the principle of strengthening the curtain walls and reproducing towers along their length, that is, moving the great tower from the middle of the bailey, reducing its size and putting it into the wall itself and multiplying it. This was the beginning of the castle with curtain and flanking towers, one of the earliest of which was Framlingham in Suffolk. It was erected on a more primitive structure that had been pulled down by Henry II, and it was built in about 1190 by Roger Bigod, son of the Hugh Bigod who had had his wings clipped by Henry II's advanced castle at Orford. Framlingham had a strong curtain protected all the way round by rectangular mural or flanking towers which were stronger than the wall itself, and so positioned that each one covered a sector of wall well within the range of accurate fire of arrows and other weapons and also covered the next tower. The curtain also protected the multiplying buildings inside the bailey which began at this time to house whole communities. Curtains needed to be higher than those that had surrounded the great towers and some of the new ones were as much as 40ft high.

The curtain towers were in effect great towers in miniature. As in a great tower, the ground floor was accessible from the bailey but the higher floors were barred and could only be reached by climbing one staircase and proceeding along the parapet walkway just behind the crenellations which passed through each tower and which could be shut off from the parapet. This arrangement made the towers self-contained units, so that if one fell to a besieger the whole system did not need to collapse. Each had to be taken separately. Another advantage of the towers was that they had command of the berm, that is, the sloping bank outside, and defenders could effectively deal with attackers, especially the scaling ladder operators.

In the thirteenth century military architects began to think about the actual gateway to the castle. At first, flanking towers were so placed as to provide defensive cover for every angle of the gateway against every form of attack. Then the gateway was merged with two flanking towers moved closer together to produce a fortified gatehouse. An early one was built at Rockingham. In the great Edwardian Welsh castles and elsewhere, such as Carisbrooke, these gatehouses were to become of such size that they were almost great towers. Some gateways and gatehouses were reinforced by the addition of a barbican in front. This is a narrow double-walled structure projecting outwards at right angles from the gatehouse towers and ending in a twin-towered gateway with, in many cases, a portcullis. The passageway was usually uncovered. Men could stand on the parapet between the rows of crenellations along each wall and could shower attackers with missiles if they managed to break through the outer gateway. Barbicans were not always the same shape, but the principle was the same. Good examples were at Goodrich in Herefordshire and Warwick, both of them of fourteenth-century origin.

CONCENTRIC CASTLES

The high point in castle building in Britain was reached when in the thirteenth century military engineers introduced the concentric castle. Though the idea was new here, it had long been a basic design in the Near East and the Byzantine empire. The principle was a small walled centre, with or without great tower, and with flanking towers in the curtain, the whole surrounded by a larger circumference of walling, equally fortified with towers but lower in height, so that defenders on the inmost parapets could fire downwards on attackers on or inside the outer wall. Around these was sometimes a third wall, lower still, also fortified. Ideally, the outermost gate would be, say, on the north wall, the middle gate in the south wall, and the inner gate on the north wall, a veritable maze for an attacker (see plan on page 60).

At the Golden City of Constantinople the western walls were in three layers. The front was a low, well-fortified structure. The middle wall, 100yds or so away, was higher. Beyond that was the third, massive structure put up by Emperor Theodosius II between 410 and 447. This was about 15ft thick, with an inner wall section 40ft high and an outer wall 30ft high. At 180ft intervals along its 3½mile length were nearly 100 towers—square, round and polygonal—crenellated and projecting outwards. Between the walls was a

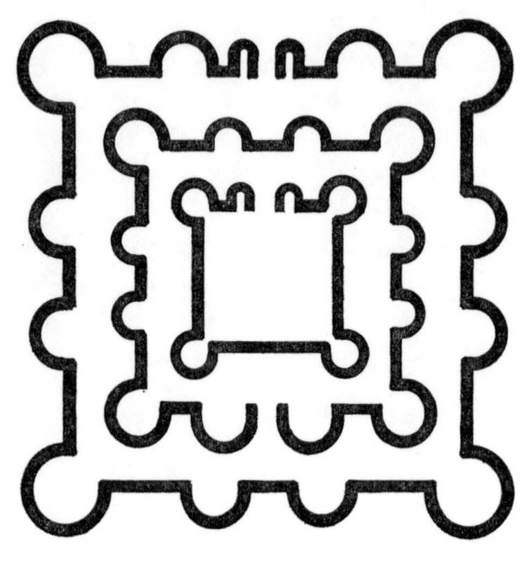

Plan of an ideal concentric castle

parapet which could only be reached by staircases from inside. Picture the scene before the eyes of a besieger—row upon row of walling, stretching for miles from the Golden Horn to the Sea of Marmora.

In southern Syria, in the early twelfth century, the Crusaders had built a splendid concentric castle on a huge mound, which had inner and outer walls with D-end, square and cylindrical flanking towers. This was the Krak des Chevaliers, quite a lot of which still stands (page 71).

With these concentric fortresses in the Near East available for all crusaders to see, one may wonder why the concentric castle took so long to come to Britain. Possibly it was the cost. Orford, a relatively simple great tower, had cost about £1,500 in the 1160s, at a time when the king's entire income from lands was not much more than £20,000 in the money of the day. Harlech, in Edward I's day, was to cost nearly £10,000.

Richard Coeur de Lion, never one to worry about spending

money, built a concentric castle called Château Gaillard (Saucy Castle) on the Seine in France. When he finished it in 1196 it was considered the most impregnable fortress in western Europe. Built on a high rock, one of its walls was the edge of a cliff. The other side, the only one which could be effectively attacked, consisted first of an outer triangular bailey, encircled by a wall with towers. Next was a wide moat, some 30ft deep, and on the inner bank of this the curtain for a second bailey, more or less hexagonal in plan, also with towers. Inside that was a third wall, around a great tower, one which was among the first to have machicolations on the battlements.

Despite its intensive fortifications and its strength, it fell in 1204 to King Philip Augustus of France whose sappers tunnelled underneath the walls, mined them, and then found their way into the great tower through its drainage system. The fall of Château Gaillard seems to have shocked western Europe, and one is compelled to wonder what additional techniques had been employed to bring this about. No doubt military engineers learned from this episode, for the concentric castles put up or adapted in Britain in the thirteenth century never fell in this manner.

One of the lessons the engineers may have learned from the Near East was how to adapt the site of a castle so that it became an integral part of the castle defences. Another was that each defence should be independent of the next, that is, when one fell, the others remained intact until each was individually taken. The flanking-tower arrangement at Framlingham and elsewhere meets this principle, but because there was only one curtain the occupants of the buildings inside were immediately in danger when the first tower fell. The concentric castle solved this problem by pushing the defences outwards and providing a series of positions at each of which an enemy could be checked before attaining the inner ring and tower or fort. Consequently, all the new and most of the adapted concentric castles were built to satisfy these principles.

The ideal concentric castle is illustrated in the plan on page 60. Its design speaks for itself. There is not an inch of cover for an attacker once he had broken through the outer gate or scaled the outer walls or mined them, and got himself into the first bailey. The same applies in the inner bailey. This ideal castle, however, was never built in Britain. The nearest to it was achieved at Caerphilly in Glamorganshire, and at Beaumaris, Harlech and Rhuddlan in North Wales, all of which have two rings of fortified walls.

The concentric castle depended on its walls and towers and did not require a great tower. The new ones of the thirteenth century did not have them. By this time the castle in Britain was no longer purely defensive. The improvements in design, with the outer wall or walls, enabled defenders to think in terms of taking the initiative, sallying out to attack a besieging army, confident that the inner wall and its towers could look after themselves. As R. Allen Brown has said, 'the military law that attack is the best form of defence was well appreciated by the castle builders of the Middle Ages'.

Apart from the new concentric castles, Henry III and Edward I improved a number of existing castles by adding outer curtains and towers. One of these was Goodrich in Herefordshire (see page 132), an early Norman rectangular great tower that was to receive a quadrangular curtain reinforcement with cylindrical towers at each corner and another outer wall with bastions, a moat and a barbican, all in the late thirteenth and early fourteenth centuries. Others improved were Castle Rushen in the Isle of Man, Kidwelly in Wales, Corfe in Dorset and Dover. Perhaps the best example of this modification, however, was the Tower of London.

In the 1240s, Henry III embarked upon an extensive programme of rebuilding and enlarging this formidable citadel. The White Tower, described on page 105, one of the earliest and largest towers in western Europe, was now made the centre of a large bailey with a high but incomplete curtain, and with flanking towers. One, the Martin Tower, on the north-west corner, housed the Crown Jewels for a time, and it was here that Colonel Blood tried to steal them in the time of Charles II. Another, the Wakefield Tower, on the south wall facing the Thames, held state records. It was from this period of rebuilding that the routine of whitewashing the White Tower began, in about 1240.

Henry's son, Edward I, better remembered for his magnificent but expensive castles in Wales, followed his father's initiative and all but completed the White Tower's curtain. He also began to build an outer curtain with a huge moat surrounding its outside wall, providing three lines of defence. Edward III (1327–77) added some towers, and so did his grandson Richard II (1377–99).

Long before Henry III's additions, the Tower was a royal residence as well as a fortress. The White Tower, being somewhat larger than other great towers, was perhaps less claustrophobic and uncomfortable. It had the advantage of being right in the heart of the capital city of England, within easy reach of supplies of all kind. It was also a prison of a kind, though it should not be thought that prisoners of any consequence were confined in dark, wet, underground cells or beneath staircases. Invariably, they enjoyed what today would be called house arrest (such as is dealt out fairly frequently in South Africa). They could have their wives, children and even servants with them, together with their possessions, including books for those who could read. Food could be sent in from outside. Indeed, in most cases this was obligatory, for the Tower authorities did not as a rule cater for this type of royal 'guest'.

Concentric castles came just too late in Britain to be of much practical use as military fortresses, for by the time they were completed, armies had already become accustomed to fighting pitched battles in the open. Neither Beaumaris nor Conway (not concentric) was ever besieged. The Welsh were actually defeated without the use of castles, in 1282. The English were crushed at Bannockburn by the Scots in open fields, in 1314. This change in military habits coincided with a gradual improvement in the manners of the nobility and the rise of the gentry. Thereafter, castles, if they were built, were residential rather than military, and in fact were fortified houses, like Bodiam, Stokesay, Tattershall, and many others.

Chapter 5

CASTLES IN WALES

It is all too commonly thought that until the invasion of Wales by the Normans in the eleventh century, the Welsh were backward and pagan, that they had to be conquered by the Anglo-Normans and brought kicking and screaming into civilisation. Nothing could be further from the truth. The leading people in Wales were highly cultured men. While the Normans still executed men for one or other of several crimes and mutilated many more, the Welsh had abolished the death penalty as early as about 950 and had long preferred restitution to retribution, inflicting fines and not violence. Welsh poets and scholars had produced a wonderful canon of literature in which chivalry figured large, personified in the story of King Arthur and his Knights of the Round Table. Almost all Welshmen knew some of their national poetry, written as it was in the oldest living language in Europe.

But these endearing characteristics were not of much avail against the cruel and mannerless Normans who, soon after conquering England, began to carve up Wales. Just as they had done in England, they put up mottes in Wales as they moved along their paths of conquest. The earliest ones were as scattered as Cardigan, Pembroke, Carmarthen, Rhuddlan, Montgomery and Chepstow, all of which were completed by the death of Henry I in 1135. Some of these were later converted to stone. Those in the marcher districts were permanent testimonials to the supremacy of the marcher lords which was only contested successfully in the regions of the independent Welsh princes Owain Gwynedd (1137–70), Llywelyn Fawr (The Great, 1194–1240) and his grandson Llywelyn Yr Ail (The Last, 1246–82).

It should not be thought, however, that the Welsh were not capable of building or rebuilding castles for themselves. There were many native constructions, some of them mottes and some interesting stone castles which conformed to a general pattern. The stone castles were put up in the later twelfth and early thirteenth centuries, concomitantly with the revival of Welsh strength under Owain Gwynedd and Llywelyn the Great. They were Norman in main detail, though smaller. Three good examples have survived. One is Dolbadarn, in Caernarvonshire, which guarded the northern entrance to the pass of Llanberis. Its main feature is a round great tower, even now, in a state of ruin, 40ft high, with an unprotected flight of steps going up the side to an entrance on the first floor. Another is Ewloe, in Flintshire, probably built in the time of Henry II of England whose forces were defeated in 1157 by the sons of Owain Gwynedd. It, too, has a round great tower of later date. The third is Dolwyddelan, in Caernarvonshire, near Betws-y-Coed, probably built by Owain Gwynedd in the last years of his reign. It has a rectangular great tower, similar to the English ones of the same period.

These three castles were all in North Wales, emphasising the supremacy the princes of Gwynedd held in that part of the country. Ewloe, admittedly, was in marcher territory, but it seems to have been in a pocket of Welsh resistance, in defiance of the Earl of Chester. Other northern Welsh-built castles were at Prestatyn in Flintshire which held out against Henry II, Denbigh, built on a rock high above the town before the Norman Conquest of England and re-built in Edward I's time, and Criccieth, also on rock and almost surrounded by the sea, which had two curtains and towers.

In mid-Wales, one of the most important of all the Welsh-built castles was Castell-y-bere, in Merionethshire, under the shadow of Cader Idris. It was built by Llywelyn the Great in the 1230s and may have been used by him as administrative headquarters. Little remains, but in its heyday it must have been impressive.

In the south, Welshmen seemed to spend more time besieging Norman-built castles or capturing them by stealth than in putting up their own. This was partly because of the dominance of the marcher lords. It was one thing to attack a castle, even to take it by storm. It was another to build one from scratch in what was almost conquered territory, where your masters had their police forces operating throughout the countryside. Among the Norman castles which exchanged hands in those days was Cardiff, originally a motte put up in about 1095 by Robert Fitzhamon within the surround of some Roman walls. It was reconstructed in the twelfth century and given a shell keep inside an enclosure of polygonal plan. Another was Carreg Cennen, in Carmarthenshire, a stone-wall quadrangle with towers which once had an outer wall and so comformed to the concentric principle. Llanstephan, near the mouth of the river Towey in Carmarthenshire, captured by the Welsh in 1146, was greatly altered in the thirteenth century. Builth, put up by the Normans, was captured by Llywelyn the Last and held until his death outside it in 1282.

It was in Wales that the concentric castle reached the zenith of its development in western Europe. The first new concentric castle was Caerphilly, built not by Edward I but by a marcher lord, Gilbert de Clare, in the reign of Henry III. Work began in about 1268, but it was carried on with great difficulty for the native Welsh did everything they could to obstruct it. The first buildings were destroyed by Llywelyn and so was de Clare's second attempt a few years later. After the great Welsh prince's death, de Clare once more began to build. This time it was completed, though not until after his death. Occupying 30 odd acres of land, it stood on a mound of gravel in the centre of an artificial lake, made by damming two water courses and converting the marsh into a catchment basin. It conformed better than any other British castle to the ideal of concentricity.

In 1272, Henry III died and was succeeded by his son, Edward I (1272–1307), who was away on a Crusade in the Levant at the time. Two years later, Edward was back in England, making preparations for his coronation. To the ceremony he summoned Alexander, King of Scotland, and Llywelyn, Prince of Wales, as he regarded both as feudal vassals. The former accepted, the latter refused. The new king chalked this refusal down as a score which he would one day have to settle with the recalcitrant Welshman.

Over the next eight years Edward and Llywelyn argued, bandied demands and refusals, even fought (in 1277), and then reached agreement. But in 1282 they fell out again, and Edward decided the time had come to conquer Wales. In the interval he had put up three major castles, at Flint, Rhuddlan and as far west as Aberystwyth, all to command important routes of communication. Flint, on the mouth of the Dee, still has the remnants of a huge cylindrical great tower placed outside one corner of a rectangular curtain with a smaller cylindrical tower at each of the other three corners. The great tower was separated by a moat into which the Dee flowed and which was connected with the rectangle by a drawbridge. It was at Flint that Richard II surrendered in 1399 to Henry Bolingbroke, who was to follow as Henry IV.

Rhuddlan, the first of Edward's concentric castles, was raised on the Clwyd, very close to the site of an older motte of the Conqueror's reign. It was still basically a wooden structure as late as 1241, according to surviving records of payments for timber for repairs. Llywelyn the Last made the castle one of his principal centres, but after his defeat in 1277 he evacuated it. Edward I thereupon began the stone concentric structure whose magnificent remains are still in great part standing.

Aberystwyth was right on the sea. It was captured by Owain Glyndŵr in 1404, but he was compelled to abandon it four years later when Henry of Monmouth (later Henry V) threatened it with a huge cannon, called the Great King's Gun. This was probably the biggest piece of artillery yet seen in Britain. It weighed 4 tons and had been hauled to the district all the way from the English Midlands where it had been wrought.

Edward's conquest of Wales in 1282 was swift, largely because after Llywelyn had been ambushed and slain near Builth Wells, Welsh resistance petered out. A fluttering rising a few months later under his brother Dafydd was ruthlessly suppressed and Dafydd executed. It was the end of Wales as an independent nation—unless one counts the temporary period of national resurgence under Owain Glyndŵr in the first years of the fifteenth century.

From the newly rebuilt castle at Rhuddlan, Edward issued the Statute of Rhuddlan, in 1284, by which he created the principality of Wales. To be ruled by the English royal family directly, it consisted of the six counties of Anglesey, Caernarvon, Merioneth, Flint, Cardigan and Carmarthen. The rest of the country was left to the Anglo-Norman marcher lords already in possession. Edward announced an administrative and judicial structure which was to survive right up to the iniquitous *Statutum Walliae*, sometimes called the Act of Union (1536).* This is not to say there were no further risings; there were many in the next decade or two, and these prompted Edward to

* Iniquitous for several reasons. The act declared its intention 'utterly to extirpe alle and singular the sinister usages and customs differing from the laws of this Realme . . . No Personne . . . that use the Welshe speche . . . shall have or enjoy the manor, office or fees within the Realme of England, Wales or other of the King's dominions . . . ' Despite this, the language, at least 2,000 years old, has survived, and is at last being spoken or learned by more people in Wales each year rather than less.

embark upon the second stage of his castle-building programme.

Four new castles were erected at strategic points in North Wales to keep the Welsh down and to act as administrative centres for the new principality. These are rightly judged as among the finest in all Britain. All on the coast or on sites commanding river mouths, they could be supplied by ship rather than via the more hazardous land routes. They were: Harlech, half a mile from Tremadoc Bay; Conway, a castle with a walled town on the river Conway; Caernarvon, also with a walled town, on the coast overlooking the river Seiont and the Menai Strait; and Beaumaris, in Anglesey, with its own moat fed by the sea, overlooking the other end of the Menai Strait. Harlech and Beaumaris are concentric; Conway and Caernarvon have single curtain walls with flanking towers. They were all huge, expensive, and breath-taking to look at. Harlech cost £9000 (about £900,000 in to-day's figures), Conway £15,000 (about £1½ million), Caernarvon £20,000 (about £2 million) and Beaumaris £7,000 (about £700,000).

To superintend the construction of these buildings Edward appointed as Master of the King's Works the highly skilled mason-engineer, Master James of St Georges. He had wide experience of castle building in Europe, especially in the state of Savoy where for a generation he had been chief architect to the rulers. He took his name from the castle of St Georges near Lyons which belonged to them. The records of these four castles in Wales, which are more comprehensive than most, suggest that Master James employed many European workers as well as hundreds of craftsmen and labourers from every corner of England and Wales—the Midlands, Yorkshire, East Anglia, Somerset, the Welsh marches. Knoop and Jones, in their work *The Mediaeval Mason*, said that at one time (c.1295) Beaumaris

> found employment for 400 skilled masons, 30 smiths and carpenters, 1,000 unskilled workers and 200 carters . . . in its busiest

Page 71 (*above*) A model of the Krak des Chevaliers, Syria. An early twelfth-century thick curtain with flanking towers and gate, surrounded by a later twelfth- and early thirteenth-century high curtain with towers, forming a concentric castle. The Krak resisted sieges for nearly two centuries; (*below*) Caerphilly Castle, Glamorganshire. Perhaps the best example of a concentric castle in Britain. Note (on left) one of the round towers slighted after the Civil War

Page 72 (*above*) Goodrich Castle, Herefordshire. A twelfth-century rectangular great tower (on right) enclosed in later curtain-and-tower arrangement. Goodrich was one of the earlier castles to be rendered concentric by additions; (*below*) the Tower of London. The large building in the centre is the White Tower, the first stone rectangular great tower built in Britain. The concentric-plan inner and outer curtains and towers are of later date

> period the building of one north Welsh castle employed a number equal to 13 to 14 percent of the workmen employed in all the trades and commerce of London . . .

Conway had as many as 1,500 people working on it at the height of activity, and at Harlech there were 1,000. Not all the workers came willingly; many were pressed into service from both countries. The forced labour habits of the Normans would appear not to have altered in two hundred years. An account of 1277 records payment of 7½d a day to each of three mounted sergeants for guarding workmen from Yorkshire for 'seven days lest they flee on the way'. Master James, by comparison, received 3s a day, and after his death, his widow Ambrosia had a pension of 1s 6d a day for life.

Considering the size of Conway, Caernarvon, Harlech and Beaumaris, the strength of their fortifications and the range of their buildings inside the walls, the cost of building them does not seem excessive. About two thirds of the total outlay went on salaries and wages, both full and part time, and the remainder took care of transport, materials and so on. Their expense would have been kept down by the ready availability in North Wales of such building materials as rock, slate, limestone, sandstone and timber.

These four castles, and Aberystwyth, Flint and Rhuddlan, are considered by many to be the best examples of military engineering in Europe of the thirteenth and fourteenth centuries. Yet almost before they were completed—Caernarvon took forty years and Beaumaris was still not quite finished after thirty-five—they were all out of date. Gun-powder had been discovered and although it was an unreliable commodity and not yet capable of powering missiles with much accuracy, it was still a frightening development. Enthusiasm for lengthy sieges had dwindled as military leaders had come to prefer pitched battles in the open field.

Beaumaris was never in its history used in war. Caernarvon

was attacked and severely damaged by Madog ap Llywelyn, cousin to Llywelyn the Last, in 1294, when it was still only half completed, and it was besieged by Owain Glyndŵr in 1402. Conway was never attacked in its time, but in its earlier years it endured deterioration through lack of maintenance, especially the wooden parts. In 1343 six of the eight towers were declared unsafe because their timbers were rotting. Harlech, unsuccessfully besieged by Madog in 1294, required major repairs in 1343. It was described as 'weak and ruinous'. Owain Glyndŵr captured it in 1404 but was dispossessed in 1408. Rhuddlan had an uneventful existence, apart from an unsuccessful siege by Glyndŵr in 1400, but it was slighted after the Civil War.

These castles were designed to be residences as well as fortresses, though the military aspect was always uppermost. As such they were among the first in Britain. They were used as administrative headquarters, and they were accordingly designed and equipped to be much more spacious and comfortable, more environmentally tolerable than earlier great towers and curtain walls with flanking towers. Caernarvon, for example, had many apartments which did not usually figure high on the builders' lists in England, including large kitchens, a cistern tower and a granary tower. It had also been planned to accommodate the household of the Prince of Wales whenever he should elect to stay there—which, incidentally, has not been at all frequently in the 700 years since the Statute of Rhuddlan.

In the south, Caerphilly Castle, built by a marcher lord, was untroubled during the Edwardian wars, but it endured several sieges in the fourteenth century. Carreg Cennen, built some 900ft above sea level by the Welsh and occupied on and off until Edward I's forces took it in 1283, remained unhurt thereafter for a century or so until Owain Glyndŵr captured it. At Builth Wells, in Brecknockshire, the Normans had put up a castle in the twelfth century. It was seized by Llywelyn the Last in about 1260 when Henry III was King of England

and Llywelyn held it until his death in 1282. During the last struggle with the English, the Welsh prince was driven out of North Wales, and he rushed down to Brecknock to raise fresh troops to carry on the fight. Builth Castle he believed was still loyal to him, but to his horror he found that the occupants were wavering and threatening to throw in their lot with Edward. Llywelyn begged them to help but they refused. He fled into the hills and was spotted by an English infantryman, Adam Frankton, who threw a spear and killed him.

After the collapse of Llywelyn's cause, the need for castles in Wales decreased from the military view point, though they were needed for administration. This decline in military use coincided with a decline of castle use in England.

Chapter 6

CHIVALRY

We have seen that the Normans did not understand the meaning we associate with the word chivalry. Their policy, in the first years of the occupation of England, was one of oppression and division, a kind of apartheid in which the Anglo-Saxon had few rights and could expect no mercy if caught breaking any of the string of new and draconian laws which were introduced. This separatist policy was reversed, however, in the time of Henry I (1100–35) who, much more than his father the Conqueror or his brother Rufus (1087–1100), realised the advantages of combining with the native people of England and striving to build a worthy kingdom which might bear comparison with those in western Europe. Henry was nicknamed Beauclerk, and not without good reason, for he was an educated man, and his ability to read and write enabled him to get on well with the Anglo-Saxon scholars and clerics, as well as his own Norman ones. He often used to say that an illiterate king is a crowned ass, and he said it more than once in the presence of the Conqueror who could not write.

To emphasise this change in policy Henry encouraged his nobles to co-operate with the Anglo-Saxons, even to the point of taking Anglo-Saxon wives, and he set an example by marrying Matilda, daughter of Malcolm III, King of Scotland and his wife, Margaret, who was a direct descendant of Alfred the Great. This fusion of Norman and Anglo-Saxon was, however, a gradual process, and it was made more so by the 'nineteen long winters' of civil war in the reign of Stephen

(1135–54), those terrible years when, as the Peterborough monk who penned the last entries in the *Anglo-Saxon Chronicle* bemoaned,

> every great man built himself castles and held them against the king . . . never did a country endure greater misery . . . and men said openly that Christ slept and his saints . . .

After the accession of the first Plantagenet king, Henry II (1154–89), the process of amalgamation continued to produce a new generation of Anglo-Normans in whom the more martial characteristics of the Normans were tempered with the gentler and more idealistic nature of the English, a people to whom the spirit of chivalry would appeal and in whom it would find expression. Many of these men flocked in great numbers to join Richard I (1189–99) in the Third Crusade against Islam in the Holy Land. Richard is said to have recruited many thousands of men from England and Wales, and while many were motivated by greed, they were also moved by finer considerations such as the cause of Christianity, the lure of adventure in a part of the world which not a few of them had heard of only in legendary accounts, and chivalry itself.

The word chivalry comes from the French *chevalerie* which means knighthood. In the early years of the eleventh century, a knight was hardly more than an ordinary soldier, fighting on foot or on horseback. He lived with the lord as a relatively unimportant member of the household, though he was considered a valuable asset in battle. After the Conquest, in which knights played a vital role, many were given lands as tenants (fiefs) in payment for services, and this made them more important. Some became minor lords, with their own subtenants and serfs. Following the custom in Normandy—as well as in Anglo-Saxon England—they were expected to serve forty days every year in army training or in castle guard duty. In war they were obliged to serve for as long as two months on horseback at their own expense, to provide their own horse as well as feed it, and, if possible, to pay also for a packhorse and a squire.

Over the years this simple conception of knighthood developed into something much more complex. It came to mean a code of behaviour not only in the field but also in everyday life, and it was followed by an increasingly select class of people. A knight became a gentleman on horseback. He was usually, though not always, of noble birth. The bestowal of knighthood also came to be surrounded with elaborate ritual. A boy who was singled out for eventual knighthood was taken away from his home at the age of seven and sent to a lord's castle. There he was put to a range of duties. One of these was waiting on the womenfolk. This was to get him accustomed to respecting women and to encourage good manners in general, for devotion to women and a readiness to help them in any kind of trouble were principal knightly virtues. He had lessons in Latin and in European languages, and he was taught music and singing and rhyming. He also spent many hours in a variety of physical exercises and games.

At fourteen, the boy, if he had passed his 'apprenticeship' satisfactorily, became a squire and at once started to learn all about arms, armour and weapon drill, how to ride, jump, swim, hunt and joust. He served the lord in his chamber or in the great hall at meal times, where he might taste the food. He learned to groom a horse and how to make, sharpen and repair weapons, under instruction from resident blacksmiths, so that he could forge weapons in time of war. If he was ordered to accompany his lord in battle he had more duties in the field helping the lord or another fully armoured knight up on to his horse, or in looking after captives.

At his majority, the boy would receive the accolade, a word taken from the French *colée* which meant a chop on the side of the neck. This would be conferred by the king or an army commander if the knighthood was earned on the field. When it was not on the field, it was usually bestowed at public functions or at a coronation or important wedding. Young would-be knights, however, longed for the accolade on the battlefield, as it was one of the highest aspirations of the man of chivalry.

In the fourteenth century the first of the orders of chivalry was created by Edward III (1327–77), the victor of Crécy, in 1348. It was intended as a reward for his field commanders and also to collect around him a gathering of good knights and companions. This was the Order of the Garter. It was dedicated to St George, and it had twenty-six members in addition to himself. They were joined together by promises of eternal friendship.

> Tie about thy leg for thy renown this noble Garter, wear it as the symbol of the most illustrious Order, never to be forgotten or laid aside, that thereby thou mayest be admonished to be courageous, and, having undertaken a just war . . . stand firm and valiantly and successfully conquer . . .

So ran the enjoinder at the installation of each knight. The order included Edward Plantagenet, the Black Prince, the king's eldest son, not yet twenty but already the most talked-about knight in Europe. This ancient order is now the senior order of chivalry in Britain and is accepted as the leading order in the world. The ceremony of bestowal was a complex one, evocative, and symbolic of the conception of King Arthur and his Knights of the Round Table. At first, indeed, Edward had intended to dedicate the order to Arthur.

Another order, instituted in England at the end of the fourteenth century, was the Order of the Bath. The ceremony, in which the recipient was immersed in a bath and then clothed with a red coat and mantle with white coif and girdle, had much Christian significance. The knight was meant to come from his bath as free from sin as a baby from the font of baptism.

The red of the mantle symbolised his blood which he was to give if required in the service of the Church, and the white girdle was to be a reminder that he was to keep his body pure.

These and many other medieval orders which followed emphasised the ideals of knighthood, prowess and loyalty, to which were added the devotion to women, a disregard for wealth, frankness of manner, comradeship even with one's enemies, and good behaviour to all. The disregard for wealth may have stemmed from a problem encountered in the earlier Crusades. Kings and barons on these extravagant and, on the whole unsuccessful, expeditions took knights with them. If they failed to pay them, they ran the risk of being deserted by them. Generosity, therefore, became a necessity, and in time a virtue.

Comradeship with one's enemies was well illustrated in a note by Thomas Walsingham of St Albans, the author of *Chronicon Angliae*, who died in about 1422. He describes how, in the campaign of John of Gaunt, Edward III's fourth son and the king of Portugal against France and Spain in 1389, disease broke out in the Portuguese camp. English knights who did not succumb were granted safe conduct to convalesce among the French, and then, when they were well again, they returned to their own camp—to fight the French again! 'French and English, though they be bitter foes in their own countries, yet abroad they often help each other like brethren,' Walsingham added.

In these days warfare was not unlike a game, and there was a good chance of survival. Chaucer's Knight who claimed to have survived fifteen 'mortal' combats was not a rarity. It was not worthy to kill your opponent knight unless you absolutely had to. It was customary to spare him, and then collect a ransom. Infantrymen and archers, however, since they were not of noble birth or part of the structure of chivalry, could be slaughtered without compunction. When besieging a castle, it was quite customary for a commander to meet the castle holder outside and parley before ordering the attack.

By the time of Chaucer, chivalry had reached its height, and in the fifteenth century it was to disappear. The castle, meanwhile, as a military weapon, was already out of date, and it had begun to be transformed into a fortified dwelling house, the original meaning of the word.

THE MEDIEVAL HOUSEHOLD

The ideals of chivalry cannot have been easy to follow, not least because of the uncomfortable way in which their aspirants had to live. There are several accounts of living in the Middle Ages, and a look at some aspects in the royal household, which should have been more comfortable than any other, illustrates this point.

The royal household was constantly on the move. It seldom stayed at one place for more than a week or so, but travelled all over the countryside from one residence or friendly lord's castle to another. Communications were primitive; few people ever knew where the king was. When the court moved, it took everything including the furniture in carts, waggons or large caravans. As the monarchy and nobility were military, the kings and barons were continually engaged in policing districts—until they were able to delegate some of this work to local justices—and in suppressing rebellion or getting ready to meet invasion from abroad or in the border counties from Wales and Scotland. They needed castles everywhere, and this accounts for the exceptionally large number built in the twelfth and thirteenth centuries, put by some experts as high as 350. Each castle had to be stocked up with food in advance of the arrival of a party. If it was a lord's castle, he had to bear the cost. When the supplies had been consumed, unless the party was under siege, it moved on to the next one. The king, staying in one of his own or in a lord's, would hold many official functions such as assize courts, investitures, receptions of foreign visitors, but in circumstances of great discomfort.

Then he would move on, his servants having gone ahead to ensure that the next place of call was provisioned, the fires lit, the water checked, the defences got ready. It may have been a good way to get to know the people in the various parts of the kingdom, but it was exhausting for king and court alike. The organisation and commissariat must often have been chaotic.

The king ate two meals a day, and these were supplemented by snacks. Food was set out on trestle tables which were covered with cloths. The king's table was elevated above the others on a dais. The meal was of meat or fish, according to the day of the week, and both were eaten with bread, usually made up in flat cakes. The king's bread which he might share with guests was wheat-based. The other people ate rye bread. The only implements on the tables were knives; men hacked pieces off the meat joints which had been roasted on a spit over the log fire, and they ate with their fingers. Meat and fowl bones were thrown onto the floor which was covered with rushes for warmth. Apparently, these were changed every day, but this cannot have done much to obviate the stench, especially as the meat was usually rotten and eatable only because it was smothered in spices and sauce. Wandering beggars were allowed to come in and help themselves to these scraps but they had to take their chance with the dogs who were permitted to wander about in search of tit-bits. Anyone who has tried to take a bone from a dog which has its teeth sunk into it will know something of the hazards these mendicants faced.

The menu for breakfast for the Percy family, as recorded in the fourteenth-century *Northumberland Household Book*, was: 'for my lord and lady a loaf of bread in trenchers (cut in slices, used as plates and then thrown to the dogs), a quart of beer or a quart of wine, two pieces of salt fish, herring or sprats'. This was for Sunday, Tuesday, Thursday and Saturday. Meat was eaten instead of the fish on the other three days. According to the Italian monk, Salimbene, the English lords enjoyed their liquor. They quaffed whole cups full, often in one go. It was usually wine, which was then the national drink, but beer was sometimes drunk. When the quartermaster was organising supplies for the castle at Lancaster in 1215 in preparation for siege, he ordered, along with 80 live cows and 130 sheep, huge quantities of wine.

While the business of eating and drinking was going on, the king and his guests were 'gladded with lutes and harps . . . mirth of song and of instruments of music . . .'

Quite often vast banquets were organised. In 1246 Henry III planned one for guests at Gloucester Castle. This required 5,000 chickens, 1,100 partridges, hares and rabbits, 10,000 eels, 36 swans, 34 peacocks and 90 boars. This sort of detail amply shows that eating played a dominant part in upper-class life in the Middle Ages, but it is hard to see how these meals could have been very enjoyable unless they were deliberate forms of escape from the awful realities of living in castles. There were seldom any proper kitchens. When there were, they were often in the basement or ground floor. King John had one built at Marlborough Castle with ovens big enough to roast two or three oxen in each. Otherwise, food was sometimes cooked in the great hall or the solar. There was little furniture. No one had thought of devising a moveable chair with a soft seat or back. There were no wooden cupboards for storage until the fourteenth century in England, and articles of all kinds were left lying about on tables, windowsills and benches or were thrown into chests to add to the jumble already there. The king often had to receive guests, even ambassadors, sitting on his bed.

How would one display the qualities of chivalry in households like this?

The answer was to build a different sort of residence, one in which comfort and convenience played a greater part, and in time completely supplanted the military aspects.

Chapter 7

THE DECLINE OF THE CASTLE IN ENGLAND AND WALES

In the fourteenth century the only improvement that could be made to the concentric castle was to increase the number of curtains. But this was both costly and in most cases geographically difficult, if not impossible. Since, by the nature of things, methods of waging war do not stand still, castles became less important from the strategic point of view, and when they did so, there was only one way for them to go—down-hill. Their decline was accelerated by several factors. The position of the king in England was considerably stronger than it had been, and so was that of central government. The need for new castles thus diminished. Converting existing castles into more administrative and residential use was also costly and sometimes impractical, but it was done in many instances, nonetheless. £2,000 was spent on Rochester between 1367 and 1383, and Edward III lavished nearly £50,000 in about thirty years on Windsor which he converted into a royal home. Goodrich, Dover, Kenilworth and the Tower of London all had expensive improvements.

In Wales, some of the bigger castles like Harlech, Caernarvon and Rhuddlan were used for administration of a nation which was more or less crushed. It may well be that Owain Glyndŵr's success against some of the Welsh castles early in the fifteenth century was in part due to the fact that their defences, even their fabric, had been neglected.

The dominating influence of the baronage, meanwhile, was being challenged by an increasingly rich middle class of manufacturers and traders, interested in industry and commerce and not in warfare and feuding. They were becoming more and more valuable to king and country alike, and they preferred to live in the towns in which they were making their money.

Chivalry, so much identified with Edward III as a younger man, received a death blow—as did many aspects of medieval life—from the great epidemic, the Black Death, which carried off a third or more of the population of England in its first visitation in 1349–50. The great historian Froissart (c.1330–1400), an exact contemporary of Chaucer whom he knew well, believed that chivalry had already begun to decline before this. Petrus Lesensis, in a letter (from *Epistolae*, xciv, to John the Archdeacon), complained:

> I cannot bear the vaunting and vainglory of the knights your nephews . . . the order of knighthood is mere disorder. For he whose mouth is defiled with the foulest words, whose oaths are most detestable, who least fears God, who vilifies God's ministers, who feareth not the church, that man is nowadays reputed bravest and most renowned of the knightly band . . . These men contend in wassail and drunkenness; they stagnate in sluggardly and rot in riotous living, dragging through their degenerate lives in uncleanness, they dishonour the name and honour of knighthood . . .

This may be too stern a view, or Petrus may have come upon an exceptionally bad clique of young men. But the view could have been a warning sign of the terrifying lack of morality and chivalry which was to characterise the conduct of the nobility, the knightage and the gentry in the dreadful Wars of the Roses in the middle of the fifteenth century.

The fourteenth century was dominated in western Europe by the struggle (later known as the Hundred Years War) between Edward III who coveted the French throne and Philip VI who occupied it. This century saw a marked increase in the phenomenon of mercenary soldiers. These were wandering professional troops who fought for whoever cared to pay and equip them best. Consequently, their loyalty—if that is the word one can apply to this kind of soldier—was continuously suspect, not only in the field of battle but more so back home when the fighting was over. 'Fear of revolt, therefore, was a constant menace during the later Middle Ages in Europe, and had a profound effect upon the plan of later castles', believed O'Neil, author of the HMSO book *Castles*. Such new castles as were built in England and Wales reflected this fear, and where possible, quarters for the lord and for the retainers (usually mercenaries) were kept distinctly apart. In some, especially those like Bodiam, there was no contact at all between the two, and in others it was only minimal.

The lord's quarters were well defended, and he could retire to them with safety if his mercenaries decided to change their allegiance. In many castles his refuge was the gatehouse, which we have seen was sometimes so massive that it was almost a great tower in itself. Huge gatehouses can be seen at Harlech, Denbigh, Beaumaris (two of them), Caerphilly, Dunstanburgh and Warwick, among others. They were practically self-contained. The ground floor was sealed off from the upper storeys so that even if it were seized, fighting could go on above. In addition, the upper storeys commanded an overall view of the whole castle inside the curtain, acting as a deterrent to rebellion within.

An attempt was made to overcome this problem of internal rebellion in the building of Sir Edward Dalyngrigge's fortified manorhouse at Bodiam in Sussex, for which he was granted a licence to crenellate by Richard II in 1385. It stands in the middle of a lake. It is square with round towers at the four corners, a pair of polygonal towers forming the gatehouse at the north side, and square towers on each of the other three sides. The interior arrangement allowed for quarters of one kind or another around the whole periphery. These were duplicated, one suite being exclusive to Sir Edward and the other, with no connecting passage, in use by the hired retainers. What has been erected here is a castle which conforms to the concentric principle, except that the outer curtain is a deep moat. It was also one of the earliest examples of a home being made defensive against attack from all angles, a structure basically for living in and not chiefly military. Bodiam is generally regarded as the last stone castle of any quality to be put up in England. Others with the same type of separated living quarters scheme include Raglan and Warkworth. Clifford's Tower in York, of quatrefoil plan, sited on a motte of William I, was built in the 1240s, much earlier than the others, but it provided its owner with the same kind of protection.

Some of the new castles, like Herstmonceux in Sussex, Wingfield in Derbyshire, Oxburgh in Norfolk and Tattershall in Lincolnshire, looked like fortresses. Herstmonceux, a square building with a wide moat, has an impressive gatehouse and polygonal towers all round the curtain, but as it is built of brick and not stone, it would have succumbed quickly to siege. Tattershall, a contemporary, is also brick built. It has a huge rectangular great tower, over 110ft high, with four polygonal towers clamped on to the corners. There are many Gothic windows with delicate tracery, and some excellent areas of machicolation. It might have stood a siege for slightly longer than Herstmonceux.

The decline of the castle as a military weapon coincided with the improvement of the domestic hall or manorhouse. Owners who felt the need to possess fortresses now fortified these manorhouses in a variety of ways. Stokesay in Shropshire, a small house begun at the end of the thirteenth century, had a curtain wall and a polygonal tower with crenellations granted under licence, but in no sense can it be regarded as a castle, although it is still called one.

There was one unusual and interesting new castle of the mid-fourteenth century, which was a real fortress. This was Queensborough, in the Isle of Sheppey. Believed to have been designed by the great ecclesiastical architect Yevele and started in 1361, it was circular and concentric. The outer ring was a strong circular wall surrounded by a moat. One gate in the west, flanked by a tower, provided the only entrance. The inner wall, also circular, had six towers, two in the east placed close together to form the inner gate. The castle buildings were ranged round the inner side of the inner wall, leaving a courtyard in the centre. It was perhaps not quite as impregnable as, say Harlech or Beaumaris were intended to be, but it was a castle which few, if any attackers could have taken merely by having studied other concentric castles.

The rise in influence of the commercial class led to the development of towns with walls. Townsmen considered it a privilege to be allowed to put up a wall to protect themselves, and the kings, ever pressed for funds, were generally ready to sell such privileges. Even when they were walled, towns were not unpopular or feared like castles. They did not represent a tyrannous class of people, nor did they stand for lawlessness. If they were ever looked upon with disgust by country folk it would have been through envy of their wealth, but in the fourteenth and fifteenth centuries rivalry between towns and countryside did not exist. Nor were towns claustrophobic, though they were every bit as insanitary and unhealthy.

Among the most interesting walled towns in England were London, Norwich (for generations the kingdom's second city), Southampton, York, Bristol, Hereford, Newcastle-upon-Tyne and Durham, and in Wales, Conway, Caernarvon, Chepstow and Denbigh. The wall at Norwich, which was started in about 1295 and completed fifty years later, at one time enclosed an area larger than any other, even London. Bristol, on the other hand, was less than 20 acres in area.

By the time of the Wars of the Roses (1455–85) many of the castles had sunk into a poor state of repair. Most of them were

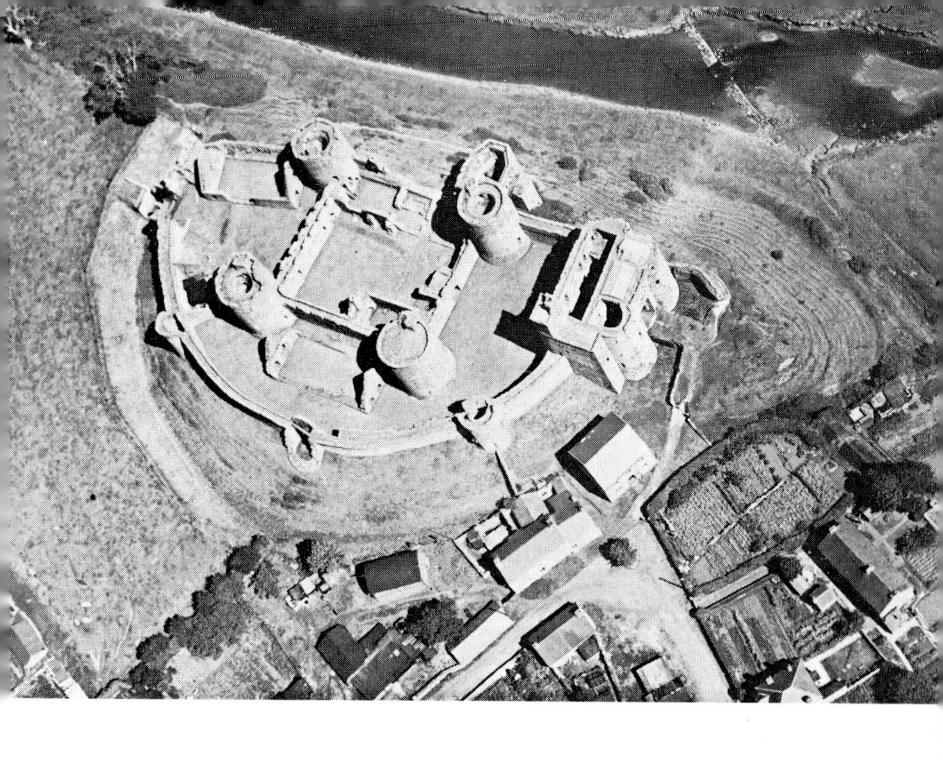

Page 89 (*above*) Kidwelly Castle, Carmarthenshire. This 'nearly concentric' castle was built in the late thirteenth and early fourteenth centuries; (*below*) Ewloe Castle, Flintshire. One of the apsidal towers of this Welsh-built thirteenth-century castle

Page 90 (*above*) Dolwyddelan Castle, Caernarvonshire. The rectangular great tower of this Welsh-built castle dates from the reign of Owain Gwynedd (1137–70); (*below*) Mousa Broch, Shetlands. An excellent example of the brochs put up in Scotland nearly 2,000 years ago. Note the only aperture in the outside wall, a low doorway on the left

not fit to occupy, particularly as by that time men had grown used to a much higher degree of comfort. Richmond had become 'roofless and of no avail'. Leicester was so bad in 1485 that Richard III refused to stay there the night before the battle of Bosworth and went instead to an inn. The wars greatly assisted this deterioration because the death roll of the castle owners, barons and their heirs, was enormous, and few survivors could afford their upkeep. The wars also brought about a severe economic depression in the time of Edward IV (1461–83) compelling him to raise what he euphemistically called 'benevolences', that is, forced loans. Hardly anyone could therefore afford to carry out major repairs to their castles.

When Henry VII took the throne of England after the battle of Bosworth in 1485 he decided to break the power of the barons once and for all. To do so he introduced the Statute of Livery and Maintenance which banned private armies and the wearing of heraldic family livery. The Earl of Oxford, one of the biggest landowners, was brazen enough to invite the king to his castle at Hedingham for dinner, where the guest was attended by servants sporting the de Vere livery. The king ate his meal, but when he left he warned Oxford that he would take action against him for breaking the law, and in due course the earl was fined heavily. Henry also made gunpowder a government monopoly and decreed severe penalties for trying to obtain it without government licence (which was very hard to get). These measures were another devastating blow to the castle, and by about 1500 a great many had become no more than imposing and picturesque but inert ruins dominating the skyline or towering over otherwise bustling towns. It was the end of medieval castle life.

The last period of castle building of any kind in the military sense in England was in the reign of Henry VIII (1509–47) who, after his rupture with Rome in the 1530s feared that England might be invaded from Europe at any moment. This prompted him to erect a series of castles and forts along the coast from Yorkshire right round to West Wales. The most impressive were on the Kent coast, in Hampshire and in Cornwall. It seems that along the coast line to be defended the king had planned the erection of blockhouses at every possible landing-place. By no means all of these were in fact built, but those that were and which have survived indicate what a massive scheme it would have been if completed. They were, for the most part, squat but substantial buildings with a central tower surrounded by other towers with rounded parapets and thick walls, in quatrefoil plan like Walmer in Kent, trefoil like St Mawes in Cornwall, or a central tower inside a polygonal wall like Pendennis in Cornwall. Deal in Kent is six-foil in plan; the petal-shaped towers carried the much improved cannons which were then being manufactured and which could cover any approach from the sea and rake the shore if a landing was made.

These fortresses were never tested in Henry VIII's time, possibly because their very massiveness and defensive excellence had a deterrent effect on would-be invaders.

In England and Wales, the death-blow to castles was delivered in the Civil War (1642–7). When Parliament went to war against Charles I, both sides immediately took over many of the castles which were in their areas of influence and repaired them. In some cases the disrepair was so extensive that only parts were rebuilt. These castles responded variously to attack in an age of controlled use of gunpowder, of more accurate gunfire, of replacement of bows and arrows by muskets and pistols. After the war Parliament decided to neutralise the castles, in case they should ever again be used by Royalists as strongholds or sites of resistance, and this was called 'slighting'. It consisted of destroying fortifications, towers and gates, and breaching walls. It was a practice that had been introduced three and a half centuries earlier in Scotland by Robert Bruce (see page 100).

Denbigh and Pontefract both withstood long sieges in the

war, the former yielding only after six months. Carisbrooke was the king's prison in 1647–8. Kenilworth changed hands in the early part of the war and thereafter remained Parliamentarian. All the same, it was slighted in 1649. Helmsley in Yorkshire was besieged and badly damaged, and so was Scarborough. Donnington in Berkshire, with its huge and disproportionate tower gatehouse (still standing) resisted a long siege by means of extensive earthworks. Devizes in Wiltshire, on the other hand, surrendered at the mere threat of artillery fire from Cromwell. Launceston in Cornwall, a shell keep of the twelfth century, was captured by Parliament in 1646 and slighted. Henry VIII's Pendennis was also taken. Nunney, in Somerset, a huge rectangular tower with round towers clamped onto the four angles, surrounded by a moat, fell to Parliament in less than two days.

In Wales, Raglan surrendered to Parliament in 1646 after a long siege and it was slighted. There are, however, some fine machicolation areas still visible today. Rhuddlan was slighted. Flint was held for the king by Sir Roger Mostyn but starved into surrender in 1643. Two years later the Royalists recaptured it, but it fell again in 1646. Powis Castle was captured by Sir Thomas Myddleton for Parliament in 1644, survived and was rebuilt in Charles II's time. It is now in a good state of repair. Aberystwyth was blown up by Parliament and is today but a collection of ruins. Caerphilly was attacked and damaged. One tower still leans over at a precarious angle as a memorial to the siege. Chepstow was overrun by Cromwell's troops and in 1648 Parliament granted it to him as a base in Wales. Pembroke declared for Cromwell but later changed its allegiance. It was then besieged by Parliament but held out for some time until a traitor inside betrayed the source of its water supply, enabling the attackers to cut it off and so induce surrender. It is said that the traitor was subsequently detected and thrown into the well. Cromwell slighted Pembroke, but could not bring down the great cylindrical tower.

Other important castles slighted were Goodrich, Bodiam and Corfe, and while of the first two there are still substantial remains today, suggesting that the order was carried out half-heartedly, Corfe is a ruin.

The subsequent history of these famous medieval castles has been varied. Many have disappeared in town-development schemes or programmes of factory, railway station or road building. Many have been left to go to ruin. Many more that had deteriorated badly have been carefully and lovingly restored, some by private owners at great cost, but the majority by the Department of Environment (formerly the Ministry of Public Building & Works) without whose efforts it would not be possible to provide a balanced picture of the castles of Britain. Some, like Warwick and Berkeley, are still lived in by descendants of their medieval owners. Some were used as quarries for building materials in the same way as ancient monuments had been in Rome. Some, like Winchester and Leicester, are used for assizes. Some like York, Lancaster and Oxford are, or were until recently, prisons. The Tower of London is, as was Dover until 1958, used for military purposes. Windsor is a royal residence, which has probably had more spent on it than any other castle in the kingdom. Durham is the official home of the bishop and the base of a university.

Whatever use these surviving castles are now put to, they remain, as long as they stand, memorials to medieval man's inhumanity to man.

Chapter 8

THE MEDIEVAL CASTLE IN SCOTLAND

The development of castle building in Scotland was not unlike that in England and Wales. The Scots were subjected to the same influences, namely, Norman aggression (but not conquest), feudalism (but chiefly in the Lowlands), factious barons, weak kings, strong kings determined to exert authority. On the whole this development followed the same sequence, motte-and-bailey, great tower, shell keep, curtain with towers, curtain with massive gatehouse and towers, concentric castle, and fortified manorhouse, though the sequence began later—and ended much later—than English and Welsh counterparts. The Scots were still building fortified houses, which they called castles, as late as the middle of the seventeenth century.

There were, however, several interesting differences between the Scottish and the English and Welsh structures. And there were stone castellar buildings, called brochs, centuries before the stone towers put up in England by the Normans.

Brochs are only found in Scotland. While most of them are in the northern half and in the islands, a few were built in the Lowlands. It is impossible to be precise about the dates of these brochs, but experts accept them as being about 2,000 years old. They are believed to have been erected by British Celts from southern and western Britain who made landings in Scotland in the years before the invasion of Britain by Julius Caesar (55 BC). Relics found in and around them suggest a high capability in farming technique and a well-developed knowledge of making textiles.

Brochs are almost always sited on the coast, and this has given rise to the suggestion that one of their main uses was to provide refuge for local inhabitants fleeing from the crews of slave-trading ships from the Roman Empire who came ashore in search of fresh supplies of human material for the Italian and provincial slave markets.

Brochs were massive and tower-like. One of the best surviving examples is Mousa (see page 90), on the rocky Shetland mainland. Today, though its top part is missing, it still resembles in shape the concave cooling towers one associates with electrical generating stations. Mousa has a 15ft-thick dry masonry wall surrounding an inner yard some 20ft in diameter. The broch is 44ft high and it has one entrance, a low narrow doorway, completely unadorned. This could be sealed off in case of attack. In the walls there are various small chambers on different levels, reached by spiral staircases in the wall thickness. There was also a gallery arrangement near the top which provided some form of protection from the elements for those below, but was probably not meant specifically to do so.

Alterations to the internal apartments seem to have been made at an indeterminate date, and these suggest that Mousa was occupied, possibly, for generations. This is perhaps borne out by the fact that it is mentioned as a place of refuge in several Viking sagas, notably the *Orkneyinga* cycle of the mid-twelfth century.

There were numerous other brochs in Scotland, the great majority of which are but ruins excavated by diligent archaeologists. One of those in the Lowlands is Edin's Hold, near Cockburn Law. Surrounded by a double rampart, it is the largest broch so far discovered. Its diameter inside is 56ft, and its walls are about 17ft thick. It has five main room areas, reached by staircases. These areas are large enough to warrant propping up by pillars.

After the subjection of the greater part of Britain by the Romans, achieved in the second century AD, the need for slave stealing by means of descents upon the rocky coasts of the north was removed, and the brochs, having proved their effectiveness in many instances, now had a new part to play as resident fortresses. The original towers were too cramped to afford comfort, and so buildings were added to them or raised up around them, sometimes filling the space between the walls and the rampart. These structures may well have afforded refuge again when the Scottish coasts were attacked by the Vikings in the eight and ninth centuries. They may even have been seized and used as homes by Viking settlers, and this could account for Mousa being mentioned in Viking literature. It might also explain the name Edin's Hold, which is another way of writing Odin's Hold. (Odin was the Viking god of war.)

The Norman conquest of England resulted in the erection of many motte-and-bailey castles, and a generation afterwards more were put up in Wales. Scotland was not conquered, although some of the more aggressive followers of William who were allotted lands in the northern English counties indulged in sporadic raiding of the border and the southernmost towns and fields of the Lowlands. The demarcation of the border itself was often in dispute. Then, in 1072, William invaded the Lowlands and reached the river Forth, though, as the *Anglo-Saxon Chronicle* has it, he gained no advantage from it. He did, however, make peace with Malcolm III (1057–93). And from then on what may be described as Norman infiltration began. It was fostered by Malcolm. Although he was a proud Scot—and had married Margaret (the sister of Edgar, the grandson of Edmund Ironside, king of England in 1016), who had no cause to love the Normans—he saw advantages in adopting feudalism in his country. This meant introducing Norman castle building in Scotland, and it also saw the construction of large abbeys and small churches in stone.

Mottes-and-baileys began to spring up in Scotland from about the last quarter of the eleventh century. The process was accelerated in the reign of David I (1124–53) and they continued to be erected right up to the early 1200s, by which time they had been obsolete in England for half a century. These mottes were fairly thick on the ground in the south-west, in river valleys like the Esk and the Nith, and along the Solway. Mottes were also built north of the Forth, but there were fewer and they are of later date, like Inverurie, near Aberdeen, built in the 1170s, which rises to over 60ft. Another at Duffus, near Elgin, was probably of the same approximate date.

Dating early Scottish castles, whether mottes or stone-built, is severely hampered by the shortage of records, reliable or otherwise, and guesswork or estimating from styles is unsatisfactory. The Scottish castles do not always conform to rules. The earliest stone-built ones were of three kinds, the tower stronghold (such as Sween), the shell keep (Rothesay), and the curtain with towers (Inverlochy), to mention three good examples. Sween, authoritatively stated by S. Cruden in *The Scottish Castle* to be the oldest stone castle (excluding the brochs) in Scotland, is in Knapdale. It was built probably in the late eleventh or early twelfth century, and with its buttresses is typically Norman in style. It is sited on a rock promontory overlooking Loch Sween in Argyll. Trapezium-shaped in plan, it has an inner area of about 3,000sq ft. It has a round and a square tower of somewhat later date. Rothesay is the best among only a few shell keeps still remaining in Scotland. On the east coast of Bute overlooking the Firth of Clyde, it is oval in shape, and had four round towers built on to the curtain later, equidistant from each other, providing full cover of all points of attack. Two other interesting shell keeps are Doune of Invernochty and Peel of Lumphanan, the site of the latter being associated with the death of King Macbeth (1040–57) who was defeated by Malcolm III. Inverlochy, a square courtyard surrounded by high walls, with large round towers rising out of each corner, was built in the last quarter of the thirteenth century, before the invasion of Scotland by Edward I in 1296.

The thirteenth century was for Scotland a critical one in her history. Much of the first two thirds were taken up with gradually edging the Vikings out of Argyll and the western islands, the Hebrides and the Orcades. It was no swift process, for the Norwegian chiefs clung tenaciously to these areas as they represented almost their last possessions in Europe. The two kings Alexander II (1214–49) and his son Alexander III (1249–86) undertook a number of projects for this long campaign, building up the navy and also erecting several fortresses on the western coast and on the islands. These were splendid structures with stone curtains, some with towers, and they were for the most part built on gaunt, rocky promontories jutting out into the sea. There, siege artillery would have been useless except perhaps against the wall facing the land side. Among these were Kisimul, on the Isle of Barra in the Outer Hebrides, Mingarry in Ardnamurchan peninsula, Argyllshire, and Dunstaffnage on Loch Etive, not far from Oban. These are, along with others like Tioram and Skipness, impossible to date with accuracy, but there is now little doubt that they were part of the two kings' scheme to rid Scotland of the Norsemen.

Kisimul, magnificent, glowering, terrifyingly isolated, seems to rise stark and sheer out of the water. In fact, the quadrangular building of curtains, with a tower at the south corner of possibly later date, is soundly enough rooted to a rock foundation. It has put-log holes in the top of the curtain for hoardings.

Mingarry, irregularly hexagonal in plan, also rises sheer. It has a massive stone curtain 6ft thick and nearly 40ft high. Its main entrance, on the sea side, is by steps cut into the rock on which the building stands.

Dunstaffnage, also on rock, is quadrangular, and more like Sween. It has 10ft walls which are over 60ft from the ground, though somewhat less from the base of the rock on which they stand.

Curtain-wall castles like these were not, however, confined to the west, and there are good examples at Balvenie in Banff (an inland one) and Kinclaven in Perthshire, though these are of larger dimensions. The latter was used by Alexander II as a residence.

Once the principle of the concentric castle had been grasped by castle-builders in England and Wales (see pages 59–64) in the middle of the thirteenth century, it could not be long before it was extended into Scotland. And since it was largely, though by no means entirely, Edward I who was responsible for concentric castles in Wales, it would not be unexpected to find concentric-type castles in Scotland at or about the time of his intervention after the death of the Maid of Norway in 1290, or when he invaded Scotland in 1296, deposed John Balliol, and took over the throne himself. The question, however, of who built them may never be satisfactorily resolved because of the dearth of records and the considerable damage done to them and others as a result of Robert Bruce's policy, during the War of Independence, of dismantling strongholds occupied by the English once they were captured —or as it may be, recaptured. Bruce did not appear to specify which should suffer and which should stay unharmed. Speculation seems a fruitless exercise. A people determined to assert their independence might be as likely to destroy buildings put up by their own kind in an age earlier and more subservient to a foreign king as those foisted on their land by that king or his associates. It is, moreover, doubtful whether Edward I could have afforded these castles in the Second Interregnum of 1296–1306, especially if they were to cost the sort of money of, say, Caernarvon or Conway (see page 142). Were they perhaps built earlier, in the last years of Alexander III?

Inverlochy in the county of Inverness was probably built in about 1280. It is almost a square curtain with large round towers on each corner. The north side is on the river Ness. In plan it is very like the inner curtain and towers of Harlech in Wales (built 1283–90), but without a gatehouse. The curtain was surrounded by a moat on the west, south and east sides, fed by the waters of the river. Outside this moat was a rampart, and this made the structure concentric. If it was built as early as 1280, then it will probably have been the result of study of the concentric principle in the Levant by engineers born in Scotland or employed by the owner. Alternatively, a study might have been made of Caerphilly, which was concentric by 1277.

Another early castle of concentric design was Caerlaverock, off the Solway Firth (see page 154), which was probably built in the decade 1280–90.

Three castles of this era are of interest, Bothwell on the Clyde (see page 151), Kildrummie in Aberdeenshire, and Dirleton in East Lothian (see page 117), on a rocky promontory overlooking the Firth of Forth. Kildrummie, now a complete ruin, had a vast gatehouse as well as a great tower. Dirleton's round great tower was part of a cluster of towers on the south side of the quadrangle, and it had two other round towers at the north east and south east.

The fourteenth century saw the decline of the truly medieval castle in Scotland, as in England and Wales. One was Doune, in Perthshire, built towards the end for the Duke of Albany, regent during the reign of the unbalanced Robert III (1390–1406) and the minority of James I (1406–37). This interesting structure was pentagonal, with a huge gatehouse complex of round tower and fort to the right of the gate passage and fortified domestic buildings, including hall, to the left. This complex also contained a lord's hall for Albany on the first floor over the gateway. But, like Bodiam and other English castles of the period built to cater for lords who had to quarter unreliable mercenaries in their homes, it was designed so that lord's and retainers' quarters were not connected. For example, though the lord's hall and the retainers' hall were on the first floor, there was no connecting passage or door. The lord's tower, a self-contained structure, also controlled the entrance and there was no other effective entrance into their quarters for mercenaries. They were subject, therefore, to constant surveillance.

Another of the last medieval castles was Tantallon, in East Lothian, overlooking the Firth of Forth. Built of local red stone in the middle of the fourteenth century, it straddles a rectangular promontory from side to side. A 50ft curtain, 12ft thick, virtually overhangs the sea, and at each end of the rectangle is a rounded tower. In the middle of the land-side wall, in front of which is a deep moat, stood a gatehouse, about 42ft square, 80ft high at one time, with four storeys, projecting out of the wall.

The end of the truly medieval castle in Scotland coincided with the development of the tower-house, approximately the same as the fortified manor-house in England. Scottish tower-houses were built in great numbers over nearly three centuries, from about 1350 to well into the seventeenth century. They were of course much more comfortable than castles, and at first were also fortified well enough to withstand certain degrees of siege. Built partly to impress local populations, partly as administrative centres for royal government or delegated local authority, and partly as refuges in the factious years of civil strife which followed the successful conclusion of the wars of independence, the tower-house 'flourished (in Scotland) as it never did anywhere else before or since' (Cruden).

Basically, tower-houses were great rectangular edifices of stone, with few windows, with battlements and gabled roofs. In many ways they resembled the great towers of the twelfth century in England, but they were much more environmentally acceptable, except from the illumination standpoint. Early tower-houses were Threave in Kirkcudbrightshire, which was over 70ft high, Hermitage (see page 153), and Craigmillar, near Edinburgh, all built in the second half of the fourteenth century. The tower of Craigmillar was begun in about 1375 in the environs of Edinburgh. In the early years of the next century an extension of one wall was erected to provide more rooms. This made the plan L-shaped, which characterises many fifteenth century tower-houses, such as Affleck on the Firth of Tay, and Auchindoun. Larger castles were also built in this period, some of them on the L-shaped plan, and some contained a tower and buildings grouped around the courtyard, like Crichton.

The improvement of firearms in the sixteenth century, especially the introduction of hand guns like muskets and pistols, led to the evolution of a new shape of tower-house, the Z-shaped structure. This was a central tower flanked directly at 45° or thereabouts on two opposite corners with towers, round or square. Each tower covers two sides of the central building which in turn covers the towers. Good examples of this type of tower-house are at Claypotts (see page 155), Glenbuchat in Strathdon, and Drochil in Peebleshire. The first Z-shaped castle was built in the fifteenth century, but the period usually associated with them is the sixteenth century. Claypotts is dated about 1570–80.

In 1603 James VI of Scotland became James I of England, Scotland and Ireland, uniting the crowns of the countries (but not the countries themselves). Warfare with England ended, except for brief periods in the Civil War and afterwards during William III's reign, and again in the two Jacobite rebellions of the eighteenth century. New buildings went up in profusion. Many were magnificent-looking residences, castle-like, over-ornamented, bearing high-pointed turrets and domes, rows of oriel windows, bartizans and machicolation almost gone mad. (A famous example of this ornament is at Glamis, in Angus, the birthplace of Queen Elizabeth the Queen Mother.) These are dramatic fairly-tale structures, but they are not in our sense of the term castles. They arose when the need for impregnable bastions had almost gone. They are often said to be heavily influenced by French château-building, but it should never be forgotten that in fact they bear unmistakable marks of Scottish national building ideas.

Chapter 9

SOME ENGLISH CASTLES

The White Tower, London

The White Tower of the Tower of London, Britain's most famous castle, was probably the first stone castle to be built in England. It is a rectangular great tower, about 107ft by 118ft, and it is just over 90ft high, from the ground to the battlements. The corners are clamped by turrets with domed tops, the north-west, the south-west, and the south-east ones being square, and the north-east a rounded turret which contains the principal staircase. Typical Norman pilaster buttresses support the stark walls which are between 12 and 15ft thick.

The entrance to the Tower was by staircase on the south wall exterior up to the first floor, as was the pattern for most Norman rectangular great towers. Inside, the tower is divided by a 10ft thick crosswall. Some of the old flooring of wood was removed by Sir Christopher Wren after 1666 and in the lower part he put in brick vaults. He also altered the windows to the present standard seventeenth-century style, and he rebuilt the chapel of St John which is on the second floor, its apse end actually in the rounded corner turret.

The third storey contained the royal apartments, notably the Council Chamber, and in these rooms some of the most momentous decisions of English history were made by kings who, it should be remembered, used the Tower as a major residence. Kings always started out from the Tower on their processions to Westminster for coronation.

The Tower is redolent with historical associations. Believed to be standing on the site of a Roman fort which may have been started by Julius Caesar, the White Tower was begun by William the Conqueror in about 1075, and finished by his son, William Rufus. This imposing fortress has never fallen in its 900 years. For some time it was, as well as a royal residence, a place of confinement (prison is too strong a word) for a motley catalogue of European rulers including David II of Scotland, John II of France (take after Poitiers in 1356), and Gryffydd ap Llywelyn, son of Llywelyn Fawr, Prince of Wales. Gryffydd tried to escape in 1244, but he fell to his death with such force, as the records says, that his head was pushed right between his shoulder blades.

There have been so many events in the long history of the Tower that they seem to justify the numerous books about it that have been written over the years. The most accurate details of the Tower's history and architectural development, however, are to be found in the official guide published by HMSO for the Department of the Environment.

Dover Castle, Kent

The supreme strategic importance of Dover Castle speaks for itself. Dover is one of the Cinque Ports. It is but 22 miles from France, from a land which for most of the thirteenth, fourteenth and fifteenth centuries was at war with England. This land is never out of sight of the inhabitants of Dover except in mist or fog. The fortress, standing on a chalk-based hillock to the east of the town, some 500ft above sea level, not only overshadows the town, the sea-port and the naval and military buildings. It also dominates both the vital strips of channel and the road to London. It has often been called the Key to England, for the first time indeed as early as the thirteenth century by the historian Matthew Paris (c.1200–59). And it has been the subject of almost continuous occupation,

Page 107 (*above*) Rochester Castle, Kent. The twelfth-century rectangular great tower. The rounded corner at the front replaced the squared corner which collapsed in 1216 (see page 50); (*below*) Conway Castle, Caernarvonshire. Built by Edward I, it has eight huge round towers flanking a thick curtain

Page 108 (*above*) Dover Castle, Kent. A fine view of its complex arrangement. On the left is the huge rectangular great tower of the twelfth century, with prominent buttresses. The double curtain-and-tower plan can easily be seen, and the castle became one of the earliest concentric types in Europe. At the centre rear is the Roman lighthouse close to the Anglo-Saxon chapel

(*right*) Tattershall Castle, Lincolnshire. A fifteenth-century rectangular great tower of brick. It is over 100ft high and it has good stretches of machicolation

fortification and embellishment since the eleventh century. It was built on Roman ruins. There are still remains of a pharos (lighthouse) standing near the Church of St Mary in the outer bailey. Then, in the last years of Edward the Confessor (1042–66) one of his friends put up a motte-and-bailey. This was strengthened by William the Conqueror shortly after his triumph at Hastings. The castle was given by him to his half brother Odo, Bishop of Bayeux, who in due course also became Earl of Kent.

The stonework complex which today fills one with awe (see opposite), and must have been terrifyingly impressive even in the great age of stone castles, began with the erection of its massive rectangular great tower, in the time of Henry II, in the 1180s. Costing about £4,000 (£400,000 approx in our money) this grand structure, one of the best of such towers in Britain, has walls over 20ft thick in places, and they are honeycombed with passages and with no less than twenty-seven complete rooms or chambers, including a chapel. The tower is nearly 100ft square, with buttresses at the corners and in the centres of the faces which project more than those at Hedingham or Richmond. Standing on a splayed plinth the tower rises to about 95ft. A massive forebuilding encloses the entrance on the east side. It is encircled by a curtain with fourteen square flanking towers, including three sets of two which enclose three gates, the King's Gate to the north-west, the Palace Gate to the south-east, and Arthur's Gate in the east. Henry II also began to build the outer curtain, completing part of the eastern side with flanking towers which seem to herald the Framlingham type of wall (see page 54) and which also herald the concentric principle. In this latter respect it pre-dates Richard Coeur de Lion's Château Gaillard (page 61) by about ten years.

Further works were undertaken at Dover in John's time, chiefly on residential quarters within the inner bailey, and on extending the outer curtain right round to Peveril's Tower.

This curtain extension had D-end flanking towers. It is possible, moreover, that John commissioned a further extension from Peveril's Tower right round the Roman lighthouse to join up with the bottom end of his father's curtain at the Penchester Tower, for excavated remains suggest a structure of this period.

Dover was besieged in 1216 by forces of Louis, Prince of France, who was invited by the barons to help them in their war against John after he had signed—but refused to adhere to—*Magna Carta.* The king ordered Hubert de Burgh to hold Dover at all costs, and this splendid servant of the royal family did so, though it nearly fell. The French attacked the north-west gate in the outer curtain and brought it down by a mine. The defenders crammed the gaping holes with all manner of rubble and continued to fight hand to hand to keep the attackers out of the inner bailey. The death of John saved the castle. Otherwise, a breach must have been made in the inner walls, perhaps even in the great tower itself. Rochester great tower had, after all, been successfully mined only a few months earlier.

Further work of improvement and strengthening was undertaken in Henry III's reign and he spent over £7,000. The damaged north-west gate was rebuilt, this time completely solid. A new gate at the west, the Constable's Tower and Gate, was built, and this was a massive structure, a complex of five towers with crenellated turrets, joined together to form a redoubtable projection along the outer curtain, providing great strength through curved thick walls, high and sheer down the face of the cliff on which the whole castle stands, towering forbiddingly even today. This complex housed quarters for the constable, guardrooms, drawbridge, portcullis and store rooms. Henry III also extended the outer curtain southwards on the western side, with flanking towers, down to the cliffs. The northern and western outer curtain, the cliff edge, and further curtaining from the cliff northwards on the east side to meet the most easterly point of John's wall, completed an outer enclosure of some 35 acres, and made it perhaps the largest castle in the country. It had also become properly concentric.

Considerable modifications were made over the next 650 years. Some, including the eighteenth century reinforcements and the changes wrought in the Napoleonic era, are regarded as regrettable by antiquarians, and these alterations are substantial. On nearly every occasion that England has been threatened, including the last two world wars, something has been done to Dover to prepare it for attack.

Richmond Castle, Yorkshire

This imposing castle in the northern and more beautiful part of Yorkshire was one of the first English stone structures put up after the Norman Conquest. It is believed that by 1075 the wooden tower on the high ground at Richmond overlooking the river Swale had been given a stone wall and a stone gate. This gate was, at the beginning of the next century, to become part of a splendid great tower. These early stone additions were commissioned by Alan Fergeant, one of the Conqueror's friends and a cousin of the Duke of Brittany. There is more stonework of this early period than at anywhere else except Colchester and London.

Richmond was an unusual castle in many respects. It had a triangular bailey surrounded by a curtain along which there were but few towers. The great tower projects out of the apex of the triangle and was guarded by what seems to have been an unimpressive barbican. The castle was seldom involved in warfare of any kind, and few arrows or gunshots have been fired at it or from it in anger. It has never been of importance in history beyond being the residence or the place of confinement of well-known people. It does not even dominate any important route of communication.

The great tower was built at the beginning of the twelfth century by Alan Fergeant's brother, Stephen. It is about 50ft square, and is over 100ft tall, with pilaster buttresses but no splayed plinth. The exterior is in good condition and much of the crenellation at the top has survived. It has some interesting features. In the basement is a fine arch leading into the bailey, and this arch is part of the earlier stone gatehouse. Upstairs, the first and second storeys and second storey and battlement level are connected by straight flights of stairs, not as with most other towers spiral staircases. The steps are in remarkably good condition but this does not detract from the exceedingly exhausting experience of climbing to the top. There, the four turrets each have two levels, and from the top you get a wonderful view of the countryside around.

Spanning outwards left and right from the great tower are the castle walls, much of them in original herringbone-pattern masonry built by Alan the Red, especially the eastern wall. This is flanked by three towers of rectangular plan. The first is romantically called the Robin Hood Tower, possibly because the castle was at one time connected with Randolf, Earl of Chester, supposedly an associate of Robin, early in the thirteenth century. Piers the Plowman has the couplet 'I cannot perfitly my pater noster as the prest he sayeth it, but I can rymes of Robin Hood and Randolf, Earl of Chestre.'

Here, the bold but impetuous Scottish king, William the Lion (1165–1214), was imprisoned for a short while on his way to Falaise in Normandy whence Henry II had him conveyed after his defeat at Alnwick. This tower is three-storeyed, the lowest one being a chapel.

At the end of the eastern wall is the Gold Hole Tower, so-called because of a tradition that it contained buried treasure, but in reality the place for some of the castle garderobes. Inside the wall at this point is what is left of Scolland's Hall, a banqueting hall named after one Scolland, dishtaster to the first Earl of Richmond. It is a good example of a great hall, some of it having been built at the end of the eleventh century.

It is sad to relate that what must in its heyday have been a splendid structure was allowed to decay so early in its history and continue to so thereafter. In the 1340s it was described as needing many repairs to walls and buildings. Two centuries later Leland called it a ruin. After that time, only desultory attempts were made to carry out repairs until at the beginning of this century the Commissioners of Works took on the task of restoration, which has since been done with great skill and care.

Restormel Castle, Cornwall

Restormel is a fine example of an early stone-built shell keep (see page 34). Sited on a spur of the river Fowey, about 1½ miles from Lostwithiel, its present condition is such that we can get a good idea of what it was like without too much guesswork.

It was built in stages. The first was a motte put up in the early twelfth century by Baldwin Fitz Turstin. It is thought that the wooden motte was soon afterwards complemented with a stone gatehouse (like Richmond, page 111) which survives today. If this were so, then the gatehouse was among the earliest in England.

About a century later, the walls of the motte were replaced by a stone wall about 25ft high and 8ft thick, with a crenellated parapet, to form a shell keep. Inside the keep, which is about 125ft across, were ranged various buildings around the inner face of the wall, two storeys high, forming a courtyard in the middle. Starting clockwise from the gatehouse at the west point, the top-floor rooms were guest rooms, garderobe, bedrooms, small chapel, solar, great hall, larder, kitchen and, another garderobe. The lower floor was storehouses, stables (near the gatehouse) and armouries. Flights of steps up to the parapet were placed on either side of the gatehouse.

The shell was built of slates probably quarried locally, for there are signs of excavation on the hill nearby. This was dressed in whitish stone. The keep was enclosed by a moat about 50ft wide, which was crossed by a drawbridge on chains falling from the gatehouse. The gatehouse was restored in the thirteenth century and made safer by two wall extensions.

Restormel does not seem to have had any strategic importance. For about two centuries it belonged to the de Cardinan family, and then it passed to Richard, Earl of Cornwall, in about 1270. He was the second son of King John and had been elected King of the Romans in 1256. He supported his brother Henry III in the war with Simon de Montfort, the founder of Parliament. He died in 1272 and his son, Henry, inherited it. When the earldom of Cornwall reverted to the Crown in 1299, Restormel went with it, and it is still part of the Duchy of Cornwall estates today. Apart from visits by Edward the Black Prince and a brief garrisoning and capture in the Civil War, its history has been uneventful. It is nonetheless an excellent example of the shell keep principle.

Orford Castle, Suffolk

Orford great tower—all that is left of Orford Castle, stands gaunt, lonely and spectacular in what was once its bailey, about half a mile from Orford quay, on the Suffolk river Alde. It overlooks the North Sea and casts its shadow across the countryside around Woodbridge. When it was built between 1165 and 1173 it was in advance of any other great tower in England, and the king, Henry II, erected it partly for coastal defence and partly to discourage Hugh Bigod, Earl of Norfolk, from treasonable activities.

The chief claim of Orford to modernity in its time was that it broke away from the contemporary rectangular great tower design and was instead polygonal (or multangular) in plan on the exterior, and cylindrical in plan on the inside. It had, including three rectangular projecting buttress-type turrets which were spaced equidistantly, twenty-one sides. It made a distinct transition between the square of Hedingham and the cylindrical of Pembroke. It had all the advantages of a cylinder tower, and it had the additional one of providing from the turrets scope for fire in every direction against attackers.

Orford was advanced also in internal appointments, which included kitchens, garderobes of a more private nature, bedrooms, cisterns and drains. It had three main storeys. The basement contained a well right in the centre of the floor, a ventilation shaft and a prison. The first floor, to which access was obtained via a staircase beginning outside and leading into a forebuilding, was a circular hall, with kitchens, chambers and garderobes leading off. These smaller rooms were actually situated in the structure of two of the three turrets, and the third turret (the south one) contained the spiral staircase, all the way from the basement to the top.

The second floor was the upper hall, with a gabled roof projecting into the battlement area where there were three turret tops. Off the upper hall were more chambers, closets, garderobes and yet another kitchen. Henry II was fond of his kitchens and had them built or added in other castles too, such as Arundel and Windsor. Inside the turret tops the builders had provided rooms for shelter from the north and east winds and even ovens for the look-outs to keep their food warm.

This remarkable great tower (see page 53) was surrounded at the time by a curtain wall with rectangular flanking towers, an interesting feature already adopted at Dover and about to be a major feature at Framlingham. Orford cost about £1,400.

Hardly had the castle been completed when it had to be used precisely for the reason for which it was erected, namely, the crushing of rebellion involving Hugh Bigod. In this rising, one of the first of the many against the king organised by one or other of his factious and impatient sons who would not wait for their inheritances, Bigod had been suborned by Prince Henry. He arranged for a force of mercenaries to come over to Suffolk from the Low Countries and land near Orford.

The presence of the king at Orford, however, helped to disaffect some of Bigod's adherents and in a short time the king crushed the revolt. Hugh's castles in East Anglia, including an earth and wood motte at Framlingham, were dismantled. Orford proved its value, and it did so again both in Richard I's and John's reigns. When the nobles rose against John after *Magna Carta*, the king sent an army to Orford under his friend Saveric de Manleon, to clear that part of the countryside of rebels. Evidently, this proved too difficult, for he had to come to Suffolk himself and in one of his rare moments of energy and dash—in such moments he proved the superior of both his father and his brother—he defeated his enemies and captured, among other places, the newly built stone castle at Framlingham (see page 54). John died, however, and within weeks all his gains, including Orford and Hedingham, fell to Louis of France.

Orford remained a royal fortress for about two centuries, with short intervals when the Bigod family captured it during the war between Henry III and Simon de Montfort. In the fourteenth century it was leased to private owners and its active history came to an end.

Framlingham Castle, Suffolk

In Chapter 4 mention was made of Framlingham as an outstanding example of castles with a curtain wall and flanking towers. These were being built in Britain from about the last two decades of the twelfth century and they were a practical alternative to great towers inside walled baileys. From the strategic viewpoint, Framlingham was not of major importance.

Page 117 (*above*) Dirleton Castle, East Lothian. Part of the cluster of towers in the region of the entrance; (*below*) Tantallon Castle, East Lothian. This rectangular curtain with flanking towers straddles the promontory jutting into the sea

Page 118 (*left*) Raglan Castle, Monmouthshire. The hexagonal-towered gatehouse of this fifteenth-century castle has well-defined machicolation on the tower parapets

(*right*) Caernarvon Castle. This photograph shows not only the complete outline of the curtain-with-flanking-towers castle, but also the walled part of the town behind it. The town was reached from the castle by the King's Gate in the centre of the northern wall of the castle

Page 119 (*above*) Dolbadarn Castle, Caernarvonshire. The round great tower of this Welsh-built castle at the pass of Llanberis. Note the square projection containing a chamber and garderobe (page 146); (*below*) Harlech Castle, Merionethshire, another Edwardian concentric castle. This one is noted for its huge gatehouse in the foreground

Page 120 (*above*) Caerlaverock Castle, Dumfries. The huge gatehouse, with its narrow entrance, is at the apex of this concentric-type castle in triangular plan. The machicolations are fifteenth century; (*below*) Claypotts Castle, Angus. One of the best examples of a Z-plan tower-house built in the sixteenth century. The gun-loops can be seen at the bottom of the walls

It was perhaps more a castle of prestige. Built by Roger Bigod, Hugh Bigod's son, in the last ten years of the twelfth century, it was erected around the remains of the earlier wooden motte. This motte had had some stonework.

The dating of the new castle at Framlingham is interesting. Henry II, the scourge of the baronage, had died. His much overrated son Richard Coeur de Lion, had succeeded, and his reign was to last ten years (1189–99) during which he spent only about ten months in England. It was for the most part a time of lawlessness, when the barons split up into two camps, those supporting the king's brother John who aimed at the regency of England in Richard's absence and those who were against John, though not necessarily for Richard. Bigod was on John's side and may have managed to keep part of East Anglia with him.

Framlingham is on the small river Ore. The ground nearby is relatively flat and the castle does not dominate the area except for the town. It was in fact much more a dwelling-place, an area of buildings inside a wall, the whole fortified by thirteen square flanking towers around the wall and built as part of it, and further fortified by ditches, ramparts and ponds outside.

The walls are substantial, about 44ft high and 8ft thick, with a crenellated exterior parapet protecting a wall walk which today does not go round the whole circumference. Inside the walls, various buildings were put up from time to time in the Middle Ages, notably a great hall between the tenth and eleventh towers (north-western) erected by Roger Bigod. Opposite, on the eastern side, between towers six and seven, are the ruins of an earlier hall which may have been built by Hugh in the 1160s, which would make this the earliest stone part of the whole castle.

The area inside the curtain is approximately 5,000sq ft, quite large enough to house an entire community or village of people, their livestock, tents, wooden shacks and so on.

The curtain's thirteen towers, tracing them in an anti-clockwise direction beginning with the south gate tower, were all about 60ft high. The gate tower had three storeys and projected outwards in square plan about 12ft. A bridge over the moat outside leads up to the doorway. Most of the remaining towers are without the fourth (inner) wall. This was in some cases provided by an interior building added later. At wall-walk level which was higher than any of the internal buildings, the inner part of the tower would have been given a timber wall, and the holes for the support members for these are still visible here and there.

The castle was probably completed early in John's reign. There are records of his being entertained there by Roger Bigod in 1212. Three years later it was besieged and taken by the king in his war against the barons. At the beginning of the 1300s Framlingham became Crown property and from thence it went to a half-brother of Edward II who was Earl of Norfolk. It remained in the Norfolk family, with short intervals, until the seventeenth century when it was sold.

Conisbrough Castle, Yorkshire

This remarkable castle (see page 54) was a cylindrical great tower, with six fat square-plan buttresses clasping its outer surface, standing inside a curtain with six flanking towers and a gate tower with barbican. The great tower was one of the earliest cylindrical towers in Britain. It was also the most splendid to look at, its shape accentuated by the buttress arrangement. In its day it had a sharp conical roof to the inner cylinder part.

The great tower stood nearly 100ft high. The buttresses, which were partly hollow and partly solid, and which bore hardly any openings for light, contributed to the meagre illumination of the rooms inside which themselves had few windows or loops. The outside staircase, of later date, was not protected by a forebuilding. It led into a chamber in the first floor and the only light in this room was afforded by the door when it was open. As there was no forebuilding protecting the staircase it was the habit to admit entrants quickly and then shut the door at once. The chamber was thus almost permanently dark or at best lit by torches.

The buttresses seem to be superfluous to the design of the great tower which should presumably have been able to stand upright on its own. Yet four of the six were functional. One contained ovens, one a pigeon loft, and two had water cisterns. Each buttress had turret tops which provided overall coverage of the base of the buttress and also of one of those on either side. If these were properly manned and supplied with armaments, attackers on the ground would surely have had no chance from the start.

The gateway to the castle is interesting. Conventionally protected by twin towers with battlements and, at some time, a portcullis, it leads into a well-planned barbican. As you went out of the gate you had to turn sharp right, along a passage protected by an outer wall. Then the passage turned three-quarters left again and went down to another twin-tower protected gated with a drawbridge that fell across a deep moat. Conisbrough stands on a natural high mound, the sides of which slope steeply into the moat.

The main parts of the castle were built at the end of the reign of Henry II. It appears to have been besieged only once to any degree and that was in the time of Edward II. It was held by the royal family for most of the fourteenth and fifteenth centuries and used from time to time as a residence. Presumably, residents occupied the various other buildings inside the curtain, for the great tower was clearly not amenable to any long-term occupation.

Colchester Castle, Essex

Colchester is one of the earliest stone-built castles of the Norman period. Its great tower is very like the great tower in London, but it is larger in all round dimensions. It was probably begun at or about the same time, and apart from London, it is the only surviving great tower built in England in the eleventh century. It does not, however, resemble London in its state of repair and is really a ruin. Even the top storey is missing.

The great tower is rectangular, the longer two sides being 151ft and the shorter 110ft. Its height cannot have been much under 90ft. On the north-east, north-west and south-west angles are square projecting towers. The south-east corner has a rounded end tower like London, and it, too, contains a chapel. Inside, the tower was divided not by one crosswall but by two, the space between the two walls being much smaller than those on either of the other sides of them. It is not known why this was done, but however narrow the space was, it was wide enough for rooms.

Colchester is probably the oldest Roman town in Britain. Certainly it was big and important very early on in the time of Roman occupation. After the Romans left in the fifth century the town decayed. Much of the grand building works crumbled and gradually sank into the earth. When the Normans came and began to build the great tower, they were fortunate in having an on-the-spot supply of Roman stone and brick and rubble. What is more, they found whole lengths of wall foundation ready for immediate superimposition of their buildings. The great tower therefore stands on the foundations of a temple put up to the glory of the emperor Claudius (AD 41–54).

Some time in the thirteenth century the entrance at the south-west corner tower was reinforced by a barbican, and a little later part of the inner bailey was enclosed by a stone curtain, sited approximately where the earlier earthwork ramparts had been thrown up by the Normans.

Colchester was a mighty fortification, but in all its long years it was hardly ever attacked. Held by forces of Charles I during the Civil War it fell to the Parliamentarians after a three months' siege. Today it is a museum.

Rochester Castle, Kent

Rochester Castle stands on the eastern bank of the Medway, on the old road from London to Dover. For centuries Rochester was an important centre, not only as a place where medieval kings operating in Kent stopped for the night or stayed for longer periods for administrative purposes, but also because it has had an episcopal seat for nearly 1,500 years.

When William I won the battle of Hastings it was a great victory over the Anglo-Saxon forces, but it was not the end of Anglo-Saxon resistance. So William ordered the construction of mottes at various strategic points in the countryside, and the reinforcement of those that had already been put up in Edward the Confessor's time. Rochester was one of the earliest new mottes, for the London-to-Dover road was of vital importance to a king of England who was also ruler of Normandy.

Twenty years after Hastings, the wooden motte was pulled down and Bishop Gundulf of Rochester was allowed to begin the construction of what in the next century became one of the most impressive and powerful castles of stone in the country. Gundulf erected some of the walls and one or two buildings, but it was not until about 1128 that work began on the splendid rectangular great tower which still stands some 125ft high. There is a document of Henry I's reign which granted the castle to the Archbishop of Canterbury and allowed him to build a tower there.

The Rochester great tower (see page 107) is very similar to that at Hedingham and was built at more or less the same time. It is about 70ft square on a splayed plinth, rising to its great height of 113ft at which it is surmounted by four square-plan turrets. Like Hedingham you can still see the put-log holes for the hoarding and also the scaffolding holes. The walls are about 12ft thick from the plinth tapering nearer the top to about 10ft. These are equipped at every floor level with a variety of rooms and galleries. On the second floor alone, for example, there are a dozen or more rooms. There are two spiral staircases, one in the west corner and one at the east which is abutted by the forebuilding.

On every level the great tower has a crosswall, which is not quite central. On the principal floor, the second, which is in two levels and is surrounded by a gallery in the wall thickness near the upper part, the crosswall is a Norman arcade of ashlar pillars. Up inside the centre pillar is a well-shaft which goes up to the top floor.

The south corner, which was originally square in plan like the other three, was rebuilt in about 1227 and made rounded. This was because the original corner had been successfully mined in the siege of 1215 (see page 50). On the north face of the east corner is the forebuilding, a large structure rising to nearly 90ft. It is about 12ft square and it encloses the entrance vestibule on the first floor into the tower. It has a chapel above the entrance which is reached through an arched doorway on the second floor. The forebuilding is itself a formidable-looking structure and clearly the best use was made of it as a defensive building during the siege, for the attackers were compelled to adopt mining, usually the last resort, as they could make no headway against the tower entrance.

Rochester was regarded as of major importance and there are several records of amounts expended upon repairs and maintenance: £100 in the time of Henry II, £115 by John in 1206, and about £700 over the first twenty years of Henry

III. Much of this last sum was on the new rounded corner. More sums were spent up to the time of the next siege, in 1264, during Simon de Montfort's war. In April of that year Simon's troops captured the bailey in a short struggle, driving the royal defenders into the great tower. There they held out for a week or so against all the armament Simon could bring against it. It is apparent that Simon considered mining the tower, but was diverted when he received news that a relieving force of the king's was on the way and had reached the outskirts of the town.

Peveril Castle, Derbyshire

One castle which is not much talked about is Peveril, or Peak, in Derbyshire. It is not even mentioned in some books on castles, and yet it is of some interest as a very early example of Norman castle building. It was begun as early as the Conqueror's reign, though it is not possible to say what form it took then, beyond being an enclosure of thick masonry of approximately triangle-shape, roughly akin to Richmond. That there was a castle there in this reign is attested in *Domesday Book*, and it belonged to the Crown but was leased to William Peveril, from which it gets its name.

Peveril remained in the family until about 1156 when the first William Peveril's son, also William, accused of poisoning Randolph, Earl of Chester, was dispossessed by the new king, Henry II, who took a fancy to the structure. There are several records of visits by the king in the earlier years. Later, in the 1170s Henry commissioned repairs and improvements, and the most striking improvement was the construction of a typical and conventional rectangular great tower, which was started in about 1174. This may seem odd, inasmuch as the same king had just completed the multangular great tower at Orford (see page 114), which was designed to frustrate the kind of mining operations which were a hazard with rectangular great towers. But Peveril was built on and between rocky crags and layers, and so mining was out of the question.

The tower is about 40ft square, with thick walls of about 10ft. It is built of local Derbyshire stone and rubble and faced with ashlar. The corners and the centre faces are supported by the conventional flat buttresses which reach up to the top of the tower and down into the plinth. The eastern corner contains a spiral staircase, and entrance into the tower at first-floor level was through a door by means of an outside staircase. The first floor was the principal apartment of the tower and it had large windows.

Other buildings were erected inside the bailey over the years, including a great hall just inside the north wall in the western corner. It was built separately from the north wall and so has its own north side. The hall had two fireplaces and also adjoining kitchens and buttery. This hall was built in the thirteenth century, possibly just before a visit there by Henry III in 1235. It seems that the castle had remained in royal hands since 1155. There is a record of 1251 to the effect that repairs were to be undertaken to the king's castle at Pech (or Peak) and this refers to an old great hall, the remains of which have been uncovered on the south-eastern side just inside the curtain.

In 1264 Peveril was given by Henry III to Simon de Montfort, who already had Kenilworth. But a year later Simon was slain at Evesham and his cause crushed by the king's son, Edward, who seven years later became Edward I.

In the fourteenth century Peveril became part of the lands of the Duchy of Lancaster and went into decline. It was still part of the Duchy in 1932 when the Ministry of Works was asked to take care of the ruins.

Kenilworth Castle, Warwickshire

Kenilworth, the romantic, aristocratic-sounding title to one of Sir Walter Scott's historical novels, is also the name of one of the finest castles in England. Though severely damaged through Parliamentarian slighting and through subsequent ravages of time, there is enough of it to see what a magnificent place it was in the fourteenth, fifteenth and sixteenth centuries. It is, however, of much older origin than that.

The first structure at Kenilworth was a Norman motte-and-bailey, put up in about 1120 by Henry I's Treasurer, Geoffrey de Clinton. Doubtless it changed hands in the disturbances of Stephen's reign, and it may have been dismantled in the early part of Henry II's reign. Some time about then a rectangular stone great tower was built, possibly by Clinton's son. This was a huge structure, not as tall as Hedingham or Richmond, since it had one less storey, but it was wider. Its four corners were towers in themselves, clamped to the angles. Its forebuilding, enclosing an entrance into the first floor, was substantial.

At the end of the twelfth century, John took over the castle and it remained a royal fortress until the sixteenth century, with a few short intervals. John took a great deal of interest in Kenilworth. It is situated in some beautiful Warwickshire countryside. He spent over £2,000 on it in about ten years, and his improvements included putting up most of the outer curtain with its buttresses and towers, a work which was completed by his son. At this time, the castle was flanked on three sides by an artificial lake created by damming the river nearby.

The lake and wall made Kenilworth almost impregnable. The castle was put to the test in 1266, during the war between Henry III and Simon de Montfort. Simon, Henry's brother-in-law, had been given the castle in 1248. When Simon was defeated and killed at Evesham in 1265, his son shut himself up in Kenilworth and waited for the king's son, Edward, to try to take it by siege. Early in the spring of 1266 Edward began to invest the castle. By all accounts he tried everything, from battering rams and belfries to boats filled with bowmen assembled on land and launched on to the lake. Then he got the Archbishop of Canterbury to stand outside the walls and pronounce excommunication on the defenders. They retaliated with jeers and insults and rude signs at the primate. So Edward tried persuasion, offering generous terms. Still young de Montfort would not yield, and for two more months held out. Finally, the food ran out, his men were crippled with dysentery and he had to surrender.

Soon after this epic siege, which lasted for nearly nine months, Henry gave Kenilworth to his son, Edmund, Earl of Lancaster, and it remained a possession of the Lancaster title until Henry Bolingbroke, Duke of Lancaster, eldest son of John of Gaunt, became Henry IV in 1399.

John of Gaunt, meanwhile, had inherited Kenilworth in 1351, and having fallen for the setting like his ancestor John, he decided to make it a place worthy of the residence of a royal duke. South west of the great tower he built a palace, kitchens, and a banqueting hall with tall, wide windows, at the top of which was tracery decoration. The hall, some 90ft long and 45ft wide, and equipped with huge fireplaces, was approached by a magnificent staircase. From the hall it was possible to see the surrounding countryside to a great distance. In effect, John transformed the castle into a splendid royal residence, but he did not forget to protect his new home, for on either end of the apartments he erected a tower strong enough to support cannons if required. One of the towers, which lay between the kitchens and the great hall, is called the Lancaster Tower.

Edward VI, in his last months in 1553, gave Kenilworth to John Dudley, Duke of Northumberland, but when on Mary's accession in 1553 Dudley was executed for trying to make his daughter-in-law, Jane Grey, queen, Mary took back the castle. Her half-sister, Elizabeth, gave it to Dudley's son, Robert, whom she loved but would not marry. He renovated the great tower, built a new gatehouse on the north-east side, and put up a block of domestic apartments some yards to the south of the great tower, inside the inner bailey.

Kenilworth passed from Dudley's family to James I and it remained a Stuart possession until the Civil War, when it was captured by Parliament. The northern wall of the great tower was then slighted and huge holes were also blown in the outer curtain. The buildings were last used by a colony of weavers from Coventry in the eighteenth century.

Bamborough Castle, Northumberlandshire

Right on the north-wind-swept coast of Northumberland, on a 150ft-high rock face, stands the medieval castle of Bamborough, with one side sheer with the cliff to the sea-shore. Vast, massive, lonely, it is but the latest of a line of fortified buildings erected there. The Romans had built a stronghold on its site. In 547, as the *Anglo-Saxon Chronicle* has it, 'Ida, from whom originally sprang the royal race of the Northumbrians . . . built Bamborough which was first enclosed by a stockade and thereafter by a rampart . . . ' Four and a half centuries later, the 'host', that is, the Vikings, destroyed it. And a century later still, William II besieged whatever had been built to replace the ruins.

It seems that in William's time it had a reputation for impregnability, which suggests it would have had some stone parts, possibly walling and a few buildings. William besieged the earl

> therein, but when the king saw that he could not storm it, he ordered a castle [presumably in this case a belfry] to be built in front of Bamborough . . . he garrisoned it strongly . . . soon after the king had gone south, the earl sallied forth . . . towards Tynemouth, but those in the new castle became aware of it and went after him and took him prisoner . . . when the king returned he had [him] taken and brought to Bamborough, and ordered both of this eyes to be put out unless the garrison would surrender the castle.

Thereafter the castle was a royal fortress. In the 1160s Henry II built a rectangular great tower on the rock, very like the one at Scarborough but with two storeys. It is raised on a solid mass of stonework, and the entrance is by means of a passage in the wall thickness (about 11ft) into the second storey.

Bamborough was besieged in the Wars of the Roses. At the start it was a Yorkist stronghold, but it fell to Margaret of Anjou, Henry VI's wife, who gave it to the care of Sir Ralph Grey. The great Kingmaker (Richard Nevill, Earl of Warwick) besieged it for the Yorkists, using one of the most concentrated barrages in English castle history.

Goodrich Castle, Herefordshire

Goodrich Castle, three miles south west of Ross-on-Wye, dominates a crossing of the river which at that point marks the border with Wales. It stands high on a hill, protected partly by a natural steep slope and valley and partly by a moat cut out of the rock on which the buildings rest. It is an impressive ruin, damaged largely by the slighting received after the Civil War, for in its earlier years it saw only a little action. Beginning as a splendid rectangular Norman great tower, of local red sandstone, it was extensively reconstructed and enlarged in the late-thirteenth century at much the same time as others like the Tower of London, and as far as its siting would allow, it was made concentric. A rectangular inner wall, reinforced by strong towers at three of the corners and a huge gatehouse with a chapel at the fourth, encloses the great tower and includes among its buildings a fine great hall, a solar, a large kitchen and another long building.

There is something eerie about the position of the great tower, cold-shouldered as it were when the rest of the quadrangle was put up. It stands there in isolation, too vast to pull down and yet seemingly nothing to do with the rest of the castle. Almost certainly no one would have occupied it once the other buildings were up, except perhaps in the last year of Edward II when the castle was seized by Richard Talbot, or during the Civil War when it was garrisoned by Royalist troops who withstood a siege but yielded when the Parliamentarians managed to cut off the water supply.

Goodrich tower was one of the best of the Norman great towers. It was built sometime in the 1150s. It has plain pilaster buttresses at the corners and in the face centres. The entrance was at the first floor though this was later filled in and another one opened at ground level. There is no sign of a forebuilding, and the staircase had been external and unprotected. Inside, the layout was not very different from, say, Hedingham. The spiral staircase is still in place.

Although the tower is over 60ft high, and was much higher still, it is hardly taller than the round towers at the quadrangle corners or the gatehouse. These towers are 20 to 30ft in diameter. They had three storeys with rooms, fireplaces and garderobes.

One improvement in the fourteenth century was a large barbican which was joined to the gatehouse by a 40ft long stone bridge of two spans. Another was the outer curtain which because of the configuration of the ground could only be raised along the west and north sides. With a small turret at the south west, another at the north west, the wall led into the barbican. So far as possible, the final layout was concentric, but the south and east sides of the inner curtain were dependent upon the rock-cut moat for the first line of defence.

The inner buildings were conventional, but the great hall was particularly large, reminding one of Kenilworth or Scollands at Richmond. It was not far short of the height of the great tower. It was 65ft long and 27ft wide, and it had tall windows with trefoil tracery decoration at the top, which may have been of later date.

Goodrich was also known as Godric's Castle. This name

may be related to a local man mentioned in *Domesday Book*, one Godric Mappeston. It began as a motte-and-bailey, which may have had some stone additions in the twelfth century. It seems to have become the property of the Crown in Henry II's reign, and Henry probably authorised the erection of the great tower. John gave the castle to William the Marshal, and thereafter it passed through several hands until it came to the Talbot, Earl of Shrewsbury, family, with whom it remained for many years.

Carisbrooke Castle, Isle of Wight

When you think of Carisbrooke you think of Charles I, lonely, defeated and humbled, confined there, comfortably it is true, by the will of Parliament against whom he had thought to levy war. Apologists for the king—and, astonishingly there are still many—weep a little at the reflection that he so nearly escaped, foiled at the last moment because he did not realise that his body was fatter than his head, and the prison bars which would allow his head through refused to budge for his chest.

This was the last event of any importance in the story of this ancient castle.

Wight, known as Vectis by the Romans, was conquered by the future emperor, Vespasian, in the fifties AD, and he built a fort on the site. In 1066 the island was granted by the Conqueror to William Fitz-Osbern (possibly the origin of the name Osborne House in the island), who raised a motte-and-bailey on the site. Early in the twelfth century a new owner, Richard de Redvers, put up a stone shell keep on the old motte site, and encircled the bailey with a stone curtain, much of which is still there. This shell keep was a polygonal structure of eleven uneven sides, approximately 60ft at the maximum width. It was built on the same principle as the round shells at Restormel and Totnes. The difference between

Carisbrooke and the other two is that Carisbrooke is a keep inside a much larger outer curtain which contained many buildings as well. There is a well in the keep which is over 160ft deep. It was described by an enthusiastic seventeenth-century diarist, Celia Fiennes, in these graphic terms: 'they draw up the bucket by a great wheel, in which they put a horse or ass. A stone thrown down sounds a long time ere you hear it splash into the water.' Today, the wheel is occasionally worked by a donkey to show how it operated.

The castle became the property of the Crown at the end of the thirteenth century and it remained so until the reign of Richard II who gave it to one of the Montacute family (the same family to whom Edward III had given Castle Rushen in the Isle of Man). Not long before this the splendid twin-towered gatehouse was built, which contains grooves for three portcullises. It was improved in the next century by fortifying the tower tops and by providing machicolation between them. In the gatehouse is a pair of large-studded lattice-moulded doors, at least 600 years old and still in good condition.

The castle walls, built in the twelfth century, probably at the same time as the shell keep, are nearly complete, and it is possible to walk round the parapet for almost the whole circumference. This wall was flanked by square towers, some of which were in Elizabethan days re-inforced so as to take cannons on their tops.

In the sixteenth century some domestic buildings were put up in the bailey, and the quarters in the keep were rebuilt. After the defeat of the Spanish Armada in 1588, new lines of defence were laid down by a specially commissioned Italian fortifications engineer, and these surround the whole castle. They were ramparts of timber and mud, revetted with sloping sides of stone.

Chapter 10

SOME CASTLES IN OTHER PARTS OF BRITAIN

WALES

Pembroke Castle, Pembrokeshire

It is interesting to reflect that the two most splendid and impressive cylindrical great towers in Britain are not in England. One is Bothwell in Scotland and the other is Pembroke in Wales. Both are damaged, but are nonetheless wonderful spectacles of military engineering.

In the reign of William II of England, by which time much of the coast line of south Wales had fallen into the hands of the Norman lords marcher, Arnulf de Montgomery conquered the independent princedom of Dyfed, which occupied Pembrokeshire as we now know it. In about 1090 he built a motte-and-bailey on the headland at Pembroke, a rocky ridge with sheer sides surrounded by a river and marshes. It was a stronghold for the forces needed to keep down the populace in Dyfed. It was also, later, to prove valuable as a base for Norman expeditions to Ireland, and it was from here that Richard de Clare, Earl of Pembroke, known as Strongbow, set out for Ireland in 1165.

During the twelfth century Pembroke grew in importance and prosperity and eventually needed more fortification. Sometime towards the end of the 1190s, when the great William Marshal, foremost baron in England and the Welsh marches, was Earl of Pembroke, construction work began on the great tower. Curtain walls and protective flanking towers had already been started.

The cylindrical great tower rose up in the middle of the inner bailey, 75ft high, 53ft in diameter, with walls 15ft thick, at the tower part just above the plinth, and 14ft at the top, giving the whole tower a very slight conical shape, accentuated by two offsets. The top floor was covered with a spring-vaulted roof above which a wall walk ran round the inner perimeter. Today, the dome part is visible for the outer parapet is missing.

The great tower, like so many of them, whether cylindrical, polygonal or square, was very sparingly supplied with windows and loopholes. Inside, the levels were reached by one spiral staircase inside the wall thickness. Although the wooden floors have gone it is easy to see how very dark and gloomy it was inside when it was occupied.

Although it is the most spectacular of the Pembroke Castle buildings, the great tower is not the only surviving part of this formidable castle. Considerable outer defences of the castle were built in the time of William de Valence, who became Earl of Pembroke in 1265. He is credited with six towers for the curtain of the outer bailey, four cylindrical and two of rectangular plan. The gatehouse, a rectangular structure with two towers, is also of this period.

Pembroke Castle was besieged by Owain Glyndŵr in 1400, but it did not fall. It endured a long siege in the Second Civil War in 1648, by Parliamentarians under Cromwell. The outer defences were damaged, but no headway could be made against the great tower. In the end the defenders were compelled to surrender by means of a trick. The tower's water supply was betrayed by one of the defenders to the Parliamentarians who promptly poisoned it. After this the defenders yielded, but not apparently before they had discovered who had betrayed them. He was pushed down the well pit and buried there.

Cromwell ordered the castle to be slighted and much damage was done to the towers and the gatehouse. But the great tower survived.

Carreg Cennen Castle, Carmarthenshire

This concentric castle stands 300ft up on precipitous limestone crags overlooking the river Cennen, not far from Llandeilo in the eastern end of Carmarthenshire, near the wonderful Black Mountains. The first buildings were erected in the thirteenth century, during the last years of the rule of Llywelyn the Great (1193–1240), prince of all Wales, and this meant they were Welsh built. Possibly part, if not all, of the walls of the inner bailey were erected at this time.

Over the next generation or so, the castle was the victim of a succession of exchanges of ownership between Welshmen and Englishmen under Edward I. In these years the castle was greatly improved, though it is not possible to date accurately who did what or when. By the end of the century the inner-bailey curtain was complete, with two strong corner towers (a north-west cylinder and a north-east square) between which stretched a very thick curtain containing centrally a large gatehouse of two rectangular towers. Interior buildings included a two-storeyed hall, kitchens, a solar, and a chapel with tower.

In the early fourteenth century during which time it was in the hands of various friends of the English crown, the northern and eastern walls were reinforced by an outer wall with towers and a gatehouse, the western and southern walls of the inner bailey not requiring reinforcement as they were perched on the limestone crags, with a sheer face dropping down into the river.

In 1362 Carreg Cennen was transferred to John of Gaunt. Forty years later it was taken by Owain Glyndŵr in his campaign to win independence for all Wales but it was retaken just before Henry V set out for France in 1414. It was severely damaged in the Wars of the Roses and thereafter decayed. The Ministry of Works took it in hand in 1932.

The principal feature of interest was the inner bailey with its walls and towers. The gatehouse on the north side was three storeys high and not far short of 30ft square in overall dimensions. It was a formidable building, almost a great tower in itself. The front faces of the twin towers were semi-octagonal and enclosed the gateway which was machicolated at the top. The gatehouse was connected to the two northern towers by the thick wall which enclosed a walk way at first-floor level to each tower.

The western cylinder tower had 10ft-thick walls through which loopholes were sited at ground and, presumably, first-floor level. It is very badly damaged and one cannot say much more about it. The north-eastern square tower, also with thick walls, is equally ruinous.

An interesting feature was the barbican leading out of the gatehouse. This is now a ruin. The projection went forwards about 15ft into a square tower and then turned sharp right, extending parallel with the north wall right to the end of the north-east square tower. This parallel part sloped downwards. Underneath the walkway in the barbican were pits over which were slung drawbridges. It would have been quite an undertaking to break into the inner bailey using this barbican.

Outside the inner curtain and the barbican was the outer bailey, bound west, north and east and sloping southerly with a masonry wall with round towers at the corners and a gateways in the eastern wall. This made Carreg Cennen concentric.

Raglan Castle, Monmouthshire

One of the last medieval castles built in Wales was Raglan, about seven miles from Monmouth. It was a large complex structure in which the hexagonal plan featured in most of its buildings. It was begun in the fifteenth century, in about 1432, by Sir William ap Thomas, who was apparently known as the Blue Knight of Gwent, the old name for the princedom embracing Monmouthshire and parts of Glamorgan and Brecknockshire. He laid out the scheme on the ruins of an earlier castle about which we know very little. By this time, castles had ceased to have much military importance and were really fortified manor houses, like Bodiam, Herstmonceux and Stokesay, and Raglan was to be no exception. It was grand, impressive, powerful-looking and it had some strength. Inside its walls it had buildings of an entirely domestic nature in Tudor and later in Stuart styles.

Perhaps the most important feature is the large hexagonal plan great tower, often known as the Yellow Tower of Gwent. This stands in its own moat and was connected to the rest of the castle by a stone bridge. It probably had one more storey than remains there today, which would have made it comparable in height with some of the grandest of the great towers. Half of its walls have disappeared: they were mined after the castle's surrender during the Civil War.

This great tower was the first of the fifteenth-century buildings. Soon after it was finished, the son of William, also called William, who came to be known as Herbert and was made Earl of Pembroke, began work on the rest of the buildings, including the walls and the hexagonal towers and gates. These structures are exceptionally interesting. From the exterior they are military looking. Gatehouse and towers had heavy stonework machicolation under the parapets. Six barriers blocked the entrance to the gatehouse. The corner towers and the outer walls had very thick walling. Then, as you went inside, the whole area divided into two parts, known as the Pitched Stone Court and the Fountain Court. These took on a very different aspect. You could be in a small square of a medieval city. Before your eyes were terraces, open staircases, long buildings with handsome doors and windows, chapels, office quarters and dining hall. Outside the south gate there was a bowling green. Here indeed was the private residence of a powerful and wealthy lord, and it was fortified to boot!

The history of Raglan was short, but eventful. It became the property of the Somerset family, one of whose members, Henry Marquess of Worcester, ancestor of the present Duke of Beaufort, backed the king in the Civil War. This staunch Royalist made Raglan one of the principal centres for Charles's cause in the west. Worcester was very rich, but he sank all he had to making it an effective Royalist citadel. He spent £40,000 in 1642, a huge sum in those days. He garrisoned it with nearly 1,000 men under arms, paid them and equipped them. When the Parliamentarians first attacked the castle in 1646, they could make little headway. Even some sixty rounds a day of 20lb cannon balls discharged at the Yellow Tower did not batter it down. Sir Thomas Fairfax, the Parliamentary commander-in-chief, brought an additional 2,000 men up against the fortress, but still did not carry the day at once.

Finally, Worcester surrendered. The castle was slighted, but it was no easy job, and what followed was probably the most dramatic manifestation of this Parliamentary policy. The Yellow Tower which had failed to collapse under artillery fire was subjected to piecemeal demolition by gangs of men working from the top downwards. This process took an unconscionably long time, and the old medieval practice of undermining was adopted. A carefully tunnelled mine was dug under one of the corners. When the props were pulled away, the wall fell away, and the tower was left looking much as it does today. After this, the spoliation of the whole castle was continued with much vigour but little discrimination.

Caernarvon Castle, Caernarvonshire

About a quarter of a mile from the present castle in Caernarvon are the remains of the Roman fort of Segontium. This was known to the Welsh as Y Gaer yn Arfon, which means the castle on the land near Mon (Anglesey) and from this comes the name Caernarvon. It was put up sometime towards the end of the first century AD, possibly under the great Roman governor of Britain, Julius Agricola.

A thousand years later, in about 1090, Hugh d'Avranches, Earl of Chester, who had come over to Hastings with the Conqueror, and who had started the process of Normanising parts of Wales, put up a motte-and-bailey near the shore of the river Seiont.

Two hundred years later, Edward I began the building of the great castle of high curtains and multangular towers which still dominates Caernarvon town and the south-western end of the Menai Strait. Much of the castle retains the original stonework, but many restorations have had to be done in recent years.

The independent Welsh princes had regarded Caernarvon as one of their centres of administration and had resided there from time to time, though the seat of the princes was at Aberffraw in Anglesey. When Llywelyn the Last was killed at Builth and Welsh resistance to Edward I faded out, the English king decided to make Caernarvon the administrative centre of the new principality of North Wales which was created by the Statute of Rhuddlan. Why Caernarvon was chosen instead of Rhuddlan is not known, but it may be surmised that by 1284 Caernarvon was already a sizeable town amenable to further development. The theory that it was selected to please the Welsh people is quite untenable. Edward never at any time had the slightest wish to please the Welsh; everything that he did was calculated to 'anglicise' the speakers of the oldest living language in Europe. When the castle was built, the Welsh feared it and they hated it.

Caernarvon was fortress and fortified town, and to superintend the construction Edward appointed Master James of St Georges (see page 70). The site chosen for the castle proper was around the earlier motte, in the south corner of the land adjacent to the Menai Strait. North of this was to be a castle moat, and behind that a trapezium-shaped area of about 400,000sq ft consisting of a grid system of streets and houses enclosed by a curtain flanked with D-end towers and twin-towered gates. This was the walled part of the town.

In plan, the castle is shaped something like an '8' lying on its side. The curtain is punctuated by nine principal towers and two massive twin-tower plan gatehouses. The northern one, the King's Gate, opens on to the moat and leads into the walled part of the town. The other, the Queen's Gate, at the south east, equally massive, leads to the town outside. Both are polygonal in plan, as are all the towers. They were equipped with the most complicated protective systems. To get into the bailey by the King's Gate, for example, one had to cross a drawbridge and go through five different doors and under six portcullises.

Of the nine towers, the most westerly, the Eagle Tower, is the most impressive. Approachable from the outside only on the sea side through an entrance in the basement level, it conforms to the medieval great tower principles, has three storeys and basement, and a crenellated parapet on top. Out of the top project three sizeable polygonal turrets which are crenellated.

The curtain wall on the southern side was thick enough to allow two firing galleries to be inserted inside the width, and below the level of the parapet. These, together with the firing positions on the parapets and those on the tops and through the windows in the southern flanking towers (Queen's, Chamberlain, Black and Cistern Towers and the Queen's

Gate) gave the defenders complete mastery over attackers from the town side or any who ventured to try to assault from the river. The curtain between the Queen's Gate and the Watch Tower (on the north-east flank) meanwhile, was thick and solid.

The building of Caernarvon Castle took forty years and was more or less continuous. There were, however, definite periods when construction activity was much greater than at others. The first period, from 1283 to 1292, was a very busy one. Timber was brought up by ship from Conway, Rhuddlan and even Liverpool, and by land from such places as the Welsh-built castle at Dolbadarn (see page 146). Hundreds of ditch diggers were hired and put under the direction of the French-born engineer, Master Manasser, who was later given a municipal post. Stone masons were press-ganged into service, presumably some of them under the same conditions as those at Rhuddlan in Flintshire. Evidently, if any old houses were standing in the way of the development, they were demolished. Compensation was not paid for at least three years.

In the early building days some timber structures were erected as quarters for the royal family, and in one of them Prince Edward, the king's second son, was born. By 1291 the curtain from the Eagle Tower at the westerly edge to the north-east tower had been completed, possibly to its full height, along with the interspersed towers, the Queen's, Chamberlain, Black and Cistern, and the Queen's Gate, though the tops of the towers were not all completed. Work on the north side was only in its early stages, however, but the castle was by then protected on that side by the great moat dug by Manasser's workforce and by the town walls which were probably completed by then.

In 1294 the Welsh rose against their English oppressors under Llywelyn the Last's kinsman, Madog, and they swiftly overran Caernarvon. A great deal of damage was done to the town and to the detested castle. The timber parts were probably totally destroyed.

The second building period, 1296 to 1301, also saw great progress. Most of the damage wrought by Madog was restored and the northern curtain with its towers (Well, Granary) and King's Gate were partly built. Thereafter the momentum diminished, though there are records of something being done practically every year down to 1330.

Caernarvon was besieged by Owain Glyndŵr in 1402 but it withstood the onslaught. After the coming of Henry VII to the throne and his monopolising of gunpowder, the castle went into decline. By 1538 it was being described as 'much ruinous and fair in decay for lack of timely reparations'.

In the Civil War it was held for the king and besieged three times. The last assault was by Major-General Mytton who captured it for Cromwell in 1646. Charles II ordered it to be pulled down in 1660 and its materials to be sold to pay for the demolition work. The local inhabitants, however, did not co-operate as the estimates for the work were much too high.

This great ruin might have deteriorated beyond restoration but for the timely succour of the government of the 1840s which commissioned extensive repairs. They were influenced partly by the growing prosperity of the town, stemming from the flourishing slate quarries nearby, and partly by the developing traffic along the London-to-Holyhead railway (which crossed the Menai Strait over Robert Stephenson's Britannia Bridge), whose line issued a branch down to Caernarvon just outside Bangor.

The present heir to the throne of Great Britain, Prince Charles, was invested as Prince of Wales in July 1969 at Caernarvon Castle, at a reconstructed medieval ceremony believed to be like those undertaken in the earliest days of the incorporation of Wales into English dominion. This last function gave the Welsh people some spiritual uplift and showed the Crown's interest in, if not concern for, Welsh matters. But it could not hide the fact that Caernarvon Castle was—and still remains—the symbol of a foreign dominion in Wales, just as were the old rectangular, polygonal and round great towers in Norman times in England.

Dolbadarn Castle, Caernarvonshire

Dolbadarn Castle was Welsh built. It has a cylindrical great tower inside a curtain containing two smaller rectangular towers and a number of buildings. It stands on a rock at the northern end of the Pass of Llanberis which is on the route from Caernarvon to the river Conway. The cylinder tower was built of mortared masonry probably in the 1220s in the time of Llywelyn the Great. Today it is still 40ft tall. It has two storeys on top of a basement. The top was crenellated with a parapet and a side walk, but this feature has disappeared.

Access to the floors from the basement was by spiral staircase at the north-east side of the tower. Opposite the arch to the staircase was another through the wall leading to a room and a garderobe which were in a square projection on the outer wall.

The tower, a little under 25ft in diameter internally, is much smaller than Pembroke, and it could not have accommodated a lord, his family and their retainers. The ground floors had only one main room, and the first floor one large room and three small chambers. The distribution of windows and loops was extremely sparse, and lighting, even on a bright day, would not have been enough for any sort of comfort. Presumably it was limited in use to what all these medieval castles were intended for—military purposes.

The other two square towers are not in good enough condition to assess how far they rose.

The earliest part of Dolbadarn is the curtain wall. It is about 4ft thick and is built of rubble. For much of its length it follows the contours of the rock foundation on which the castle stands. Not much of it remains but it is believed it might have been as high at 11ft.

Inside the curtain to the north was the great hall, probably of a later date. It was over 50ft long and half as wide, and it lay right across the site, its end walls being part of the curtain. It was probably added by Llywelyn the Last (1246–82).

Llywelyn is recorded as having kept one of his brothers, Owain Goch (Owen the Red) in the great tower for twenty years as a prisoner. When Edward I conquered Wales, Dolbadarn was taken by the Earl of Pembroke and it was not included in the king's programme of castle building and reconstruction, and so it fell into disuse. Owain Glyndŵr used it to imprison Lord Grey de Ruthin in the early 1400s. The cruel and vicious baron was held there until £10,000 was paid in ransom for him.

Dolwyddelan Castle, Caernarvonshire

Birthplace of Llywelyn the Great, and possessing one of the oldest rectangular great towers in Britain, Dolwyddelan Castle lies in a plain by the river Lledr near Betws-y-Coed. Its compact bailey, surrounded by a curtain inside the west corner of which stand the ruins of another tower, rests on a small hillock with a sheer ridge overlooking the Lledr valley.

There are three main periods of building. The great tower was put up in the middle of the twelfth century in the reign of Owain Gwynedd (1137–70). The curtain is early thirteenth century, and the western tower was added later in the same century.

The great tower is interesting. It is modelled on contemporary English rectangular great towers, though the dimensions are smaller. It is about 44ft by 31ft. There are three floors, the first of which has the entrance by means of a forebuilding. This floor had one large room which was well lit by three wide windows, providing much more light than at Dolbadarn. Considerable alterations to the tower done a century or so ago have obscured much of the original construction, especially at the top. It is today crenellated with a parapet, and this may represent what it was like originally.

Dolwyddelan Castle is enclosed by a six-sided curtain, at the south-east end of which is the great tower. This curtain of masonry on rock is about 8ft high in places. It could have been much higher. Entrance was through one small gateway in the north side. The walls are about 8ft thick, which is the same as the great tower walls.

The only other building in the bailey is the western tower, which is rectangular. Its north-east and north-west walls are part of the curtain, and the other two walls are of later date. They are the newest part of the castle and were built not long before the Edwardian conquest. This building is two storeys high, and about 50ft by 30ft. Although it was a residence, as is shown by the inclusion of garderobes, windows, various chambers, etc, it was also a covering defence for the great tower. A strong buttress was built against the western wall and this contains garderobe shafts.

Dolwyddelan was probably one of the foremost of the native Welsh castles. It was an important structure. The surrounding curtain was built by Llywelyn the Great after he had become prince of all Wales. It followed the line of the previous wooden palisade.

Dolwyddelan was used by Llywelyn the Last and he may well have spent some of his last days there before leaving the north in search of support in Brecknockshire.

Harlech Castle, Merionethshire

Harlech is one of the grandest concentric castles in Britain. It was built under the general direction of Master James of St Georges. It looms large over Tremadoc Bay and commands much of the southern part of the Lleyn peninsula, with Criccieth Castle well in view. It was built between 1283 and 1290, which was very fast work when one considers the forty years taken for Caernarvon and Beaumaris.

Harlech's plan is as follows. The inner enclosure is almost a rectangle. Large cylinder towers are on each corner, and on the east side, the side facing the land, is a huge gatehouse fortified on the outside by two large cylinder towers and reinforced on the inside by two smaller rounded towers. Outside the enclosure is the outer bailey which is in turn surrounded on three sides by a wall with occasional flanking towers.

The castle was built of local sandstone, grey and hard. It was very formidable, but in 1294 it was besieged by Madog ap Llywelyn who had taken Caernarvon. Harlech proved too much for the luckless prince and he raised the siege. It was assaulted again in 1404 by Owain Glyndŵr who was more successful. Glyndŵr held it for four years and made it the capital of his new independent state of Wales. He held a parliament at Machynlleth and is believed to have held another in Harlech Castle.

In the Wars of the Roses Harlech was garrisoned by Jasper Tudor, half-brother to Henry VI and uncle of Henry VII. It provided a refuge for Margaret of Anjou, Henry VI's queen, after her defeat at the battle of Northampton in 1460. In the Civil War Harlech was held by Royalists, but it was taken by Major-General Mytton in 1647.

The gatehouse of Harlech is an amazing building. It is a veritable great tower in itself. Its two rear towers are taller than the rest of the buildings. It is about 80ft wide and over 50ft deep. It was a residence, sometimes for the castle's constable, but it was essentially a fortress.

ISLE OF MAN

Castle Rushen, Isle of Man

This interesting medieval polygonal castle, of concentric plan, lies in the heart of Castletown, one of the principal towns of the Isle of Man. Some Manxmen will say there is no similar monument in the world better preserved. We may not agree, but it is all the same in astonishingly good repair.

There is no particular geographical reason for erecting a castle at this point in the island, except that the land is rich and it may have been the subject of envy of greedy raiders. Nor is there any evidence of a structure there before 1066. The first stone building was the Norman great tower, built of local grey limestone. It began as a square tower in the second half of the twelfth century, but was severely damaged by Robert Bruce, King of Scotland, who in 1313 occupied the island and proclaimed it part of his dominions.

Castle Rushen was neglected for a generation, but in the 1340s the Montacute family, appointed Lords of Man by Edward III who, after Bruce's death in 1329, laid claim to the island, started to rebuild it. The tower was reinforced by three rectangular side towers, a curtain with rectangular towers, and a gateway. This improvement seems to have lasted for the next two centuries. It was an unusual application of the concentric principle. The inner fortress and the outer curtain were polygonal in plan. There was hardly a rounded wall or surface anywhere.

In the sixteenth century, by which time the island had passed into the hands of the Stanley family whose Thomas Stanley became first Earl of Derby for his part in helping Henry Tudor to win Bosworth in 1485, the castle was further strengthened to resist the effects of cannon by the addition of an outer glacis or downwards sloping bank. The castle was besieged after the Civil War by troops of Cromwell following his great victory at Worcester on 3 September 1651. One of the chief adherents of Prince Charles was James, seventh Earl of Derby, and he was executed after the battle. His widow defended Castle Rushen, but it was betrayed to Colonel Duckenfield by a Manxman, William Christian, believed to have been an ancestor of Fletcher Christian who led the mutiny against Lieutenant Bligh in HMS *Bounty* in 1789.

Castle Rushen has been used in its long history for a variety of purposes. In the Middle Ages the Tynwald, the ancient Manx Parliament which still sits, met there on several occasions. The castle has also been a prison, a lunatic asylum and a court of justice.

SCOTLAND

Bothwell Castle, Lanarkshire

'Among the foremost secular structures of the Middle Ages in Scotland.' 'The immense donjon of Bothwell, the grandest and most accomplished piece of medieval secular architecture in Scotland.' These flattering comments about Bothwell Castle are perhaps hard to understand at one's first glimpse of the ruins of Bothwell today, and a look at a ground-plan does not help to build up the image of a castle comparable with 'the best work of England, Wales or France'. The massive size of the donjon, or great tower, is indeed an indication of a once overpowering fortress dominating the Clyde, standing as a gateway to the Highlands, but one cannot help feeling that the other comments are perhaps overstatements.

Bothwell was probably built shortly after 1250 for the powerful de Moravia, or Moray, family who dominated Scottish politics during the War of Independence. It resembles in many details the fortress of Coucy in France, which had been built in the second quarter of the thirteenth century. And this was no coincidence, since the daughter of the French magnate who commissioned Coucy, married Alexander II, King of Scotland.

Bothwell stands on a rocky mound jutting out over a bend in the Clyde, not far south of Glasgow. Its plan is pentagonal. At the northern angle was a gatehouse of two large cylinder towers. To the south west, at the end of the curtain stretching down from the north-westerly half of the gatehouse was the great cylindrical donjon, or great tower, the object of so much admiration. The great tower is indeed vast and impressive. It is over 60ft in diameter and 90ft high, with walls 15ft thick. It had four storeys, basement, lord's quarters, retainers' and garrison's quarters, lord's private suite, and on top a fighting deck. Separated from the inner bailey by an arc-shaped moat, the great tower dominates an imposing accumulation of ruins of other buildings. The masonry, fine quality ashlar, contains put-log holes for scaffolding and also for hoarding.

Four other towers were erected at Bothwell, three round ones at the three remaining angles and a square one on the outer side of the south part of the curtain.

Bothwell was besieged and taken on several occasions, and in the process much damage was done. This has made dating the various parts extremely hazardous. The great tower is an original building of the first construction period. So is the southern and shortest stretch of the curtain. The remainder falls into several later construction periods, from early fourteenth to middle sixteenth centuries. It is not, therefore, easy to imagine how it looked when at its greatest extent, or indeed to say when that was.

Bothwell was an important fortress in the War of Independence. When John Baliol was driven off the Scottish throne in 1296 by Edward I of England, one of the English barons captured Bothwell and held it until 1299 when it was recaptured by the Scots after a siege lasting nearly a year. In this instance, surrender was brought about by starvation of the garrison. Two years later Edward I took the castle again after a short assault, in which operations were on a considerable scale. It appears that the king had a special belfry on wheels built in Glasgow for the job. It was made in parts which were brought to the site in thirty waggon-loads and assembled there. When the castle fell, Edward gave it to Aymer de Valence, Earl of Pembroke, who was appointed Warden of Scotland.

When Robert Bruce crushed the English at the splendid battle of Bannockburn in 1314, thereby establishing the independence of Scotland, he carried through a policy of neutralising castles, and Bothwell was one of many to suffer, though we do not know to what extent. Twenty years later, in the reign of his son, David II (1329–71), the war with England was renewed and the English captured Bothwell, rebuilding part of it. Edward III then decided to conduct operations in Scotland himself, and in 1336 he made Bothwell his headquarters. In the following spring, however, a descendant of the Moray family besieged it and captured it without difficulty. This time, the Bruce policy was implemented with some rigour. Half of the great tower was smashed down, and it has never been rebuilt.

The history of the castle thereafter was much more peaceful. It came into the ownership of the Douglases, one of the fiercest and most powerful of Scottish noble families who were not averse to murder, treachery and kidnapping to further their own ends, which were for the most part difficult to determine. It belongs today to Sir Alec Douglas-Home, but is in the care of the Department of the Environment.

Hermitage Castle, Roxburghshire

On the site where the late fourteenth century Scottish tower-house of Hermitage now stands was an earlier structure probably raised by the English. This seems to have given way to a fine and early example of the tower-house which by the end of the fourteenth century had replaced the true medieval castle. After being in the hands of the Dacres, an English family, for some while, it was returned to the Scottish Douglases, who built much of what can be seen today. In 1490, King James IV compelled the then Douglas, Earl of Angus, to exchange it with Bothwell Castle which belonged to the Hepburns, Earls of Bothwell. This family, not one whit less murderous or treacherous than the Douglases, was still in possession of Hermitage in the days of Mary, Queen of Scots, whose lover was James, the fourth earl. In October 1566, hardly more than three months after giving birth to a son (later James VI), she visited Bothwell at the castle. It is said she rode over 50 miles in one day across the moors from Jedburgh to get there.

The plan of Hermitage is rectilinear. A central rectangular mass containing a courtyard in its middle is flanked on the west side by a square tower on the north and a larger rectangular tower on the south, and on the east side by two square towers, north and south. The western and eastern ends in plan appear as two sets of separate towers, but in elevation they are joined together by a continuous top storey, presenting the appearance of a huge stone wall with a great central pointed arch reaching to the top storey. Not far down from the parapets whose fronts project a little are put-log holes for hoardings, and just above these are open doorways into the galleries behind the parapets.

Hermitage had several construction periods. The central court and its surrounding rectangular tower with a spiral staircase in the north and an entrance in the south were almost certainly built by the Douglases when they returned there in the 1370s. The surrounding rectangle of the central mass dates from a little later. The three square tower arrangements were very early fifteenth century, and the fourth rectangular tower later in the same century. The whole area is about 100ft from east to west and about 80ft from north to south.

Caerlaverock Castle, Dumfriesshire

Caerlaverock Castle is an unique structure in Britain, for while it conforms to many concentric principles, it is quite unlike all the other concentric castles. It is triangular in plan. Situated about 8 miles south-east of Dumfries, the castle overlooks the Solway Firth. It stands surrounded by a moat. It has a most unusual seventeenth-century addition, an early Scottish Renaissance-style building placed along the inside of the eastern part of the curtain, beautiful in itself but quite incongruous in its otherwise medieval setting.

The concentric castle was built at the end of the thirteenth century. It has been claimed as an English fortress, but there is nothing to prove it is not Scottish. Scotsmen had equal opportunities of discovering concentric castles in the Levant. What is more, Inverlochy, an earlier concentric-plan castle, was Scottish built.

The triangle of Caerlaverock is almost equilateral. At the northern angle is a splendid twin-cylinder tower gatehouse with a tall but very narrow entrance, hardly wide enough to admit any form of cart. The parapets of the towers and the flat frontal centre-piece of wall containing the gate are machicolated, but this was done later. Inside the gatehouse, a veritable great tower on its own, is the hall on the first floor. The curtain walls each project backwards at about 45° from the sides of the cylinder towers, giving the gatehouse a more formidable aspect than one which projects from a straight curtain, such as at Tantallon.

At each of the other two angles was a large cylinder tower, also machicolated at the top, but only the south-westerly one is still standing to any height.

Caerlaverock was besieged and taken by Edward I in 1300, an event which was celebrated in a ballad, *Le Siege de Karlaverock*, written by a scholar from Exeter present at the siege.

Claypotts, Dundee, Angus

Claypotts Castle is one of the best examples of a Z-shaped tower-house in Scotland. Work began on it shortly after the flight of Mary, Queen of Scots into England in 1568. It is in a remarkable state of preservation. Its central tower is a nearly square rectangle with gabled roof, at each end of which is a chimney-stack. On the north-east and south-west angles are circular towers of the same height, but at the top storey they change suddenly into rectangular-plan caps, the north-east one larger in base area than the tower so that it hangs over it. Both caps are gabled, with what are called crow-stepped ends, that is, an end wall of triangle shape whose sides which meet at the top present the appearance of a flight of steps.

Claypotts was designed with a view to it being defended in case of attack. At ground level it is provided with special wide-mouth gun-loops, positioned around the whole perimeter. One such loop projects through the kitchen fireplace. These loops provide for fire cover all round the outside, and they also cater for the newer hand weapons then in general use.

GAZETTEER OF SOME BRITISH MEDIEVAL CASTLES

Below are some seventy-seven British medieval castles listed in alphabetical order. Against them are some details such as the principal centuries in which they were built or added to, and selected interesting points about them. It is by no means a full list of British castles, but it does cover those which we know most about, and is therefore representative of castles throughout England, Wales and Scotland. Numbers in the first column relate to the map on page 168.

GAZETTEER OF SOME BRITISH MEDIEVAL CASTLES

	Castle	County and nearest town	Principal centuries of construction	Type of castle
1	Affleck	Angus, Dundee	15th cent	L-plan tower-house
2	Bamborough	Northumberland	12th–13th cents	square great tower
3	Barnard	Durham	12th cent	curtain with towers
4	Beaumaris	Anglesey	13th–14th cents	concentric
5	Bodiam	Sussex, Hastings	14th cent	partly concentric
6	Bothwell	Lanarkshire, nr Glasgow	13th and 14th cents	round great tower and curta
7	Broch Mousa	Shetlands, Isle of Mousa	probably 1st cent AD	round tower
8	Caerlaverock	Dumfriesshire	13th cent	concentric
9	Caernarvon	Caernarvonshire	13th–14th cents	curtain with flanking towers
10	Caerphilly	Glamorganshire	13th and 14th cents	concentric
11	Carisbrooke	Isle of Wight	11th–13th cents	motte-and-bailey, polygona shell keep, curtain, towers
12	Carlisle	Cumberland	late-12th cent	rectangular tower inside cur
13	Carreg Cennen	Carmarthen-shire, nr Llandeilo	13th and 14th cents	curtain and flanking towers
14	Castell-y-Bere	Merionethshire, nr Towyn	13th cent	
15	Castle Rising	Norfolk, King's Lynn	12th cent	rectangular great tower
16	Chepstow	Monmouthshire	12th 13th, 14th cents	rectangular great tower
17	Cilgerran	Pembrokeshire	13th–14th cents	curtain and flanking towers
18	Claypotts	Angus, Dundee	16th cent	Z-plan tower-house
19	Clifford's Tower	Yorkshire, York	11th cent (motte), 13th (shell)	motte with later shell keep
20	Conway	Caernarvonshire	13th cent	curtain wall and flanking tow
21	Conisbrough	Yorkshire, nr Doncaster	12th cent	circular great tower with six buttresses

Unusual features	*Whether besieged, and if so, when*	*Historical associations*
	Wars of Roses (1455–85)	Piers Gaveston imprisoned
	1216, 1569	besieged by Percies against Elizabeth I
huge gatehouses		
surrounded by moat. Lord's ıarters separated		builder granted licence to crenellate by Richard II
	1298, 1301, 1314, 1337	
dowless on exterior	probably, but impossible to date	
gular plan; huge gatehouse	1300, 1356, 1640	
huge gatehouses, polygonal eat tower	1294, 1403, Civil War	site of investiture of Prince of Wales
	1271, 1316, 1321, 1326	built largely by a marcher lord
. keep in one corner of rtained bailey	1377	Charles I imprisoned after Civil War
houses	1174, 1314, 1644, 1648	buildings erected by both English and Scottish kings
	1277, 1282, 1286, 1403, 1462	
building same height as great wer		confinement of Isabella, widow of Edward II
er more than twice as long as ide	Civil War	
large round towers close gether	1405	
-loops at low level		
trefoil plan of shell keep		burnt out, possibly by sabotage, 1684
t huge towers in small area	Civil War	
h of structure still standing		held by royal family for years

	Castle	County and nearest town	Principal centuries of construction	Type of castle
22	Craigmillar	Midlothian, suburb of Edinburgh	14th–16th cents	rectangular tower with curtain
23	Criccieth	Caernarvonshire	13th cent	polygonal curtain and tov
24	Crichton	Midlothian	14th–17th cents	rectangular tower-house a curtain
25	Dartmouth	Devonshire	15th cent	tower and curtain on roc
26	Deal	Kent	16th cent	coastal fortress: six-foil pl
27	Denbigh	Denbighshire	13th–14th cents	curtain with flanking tow
28	Dirleton	East Lothian	13th–16th cents	towers and curtain
29	Dolbadarn	Caernarvonshire, nr Llanberis	13th cent (Welsh built)	round great tower, curtai
30	Dolwyddelan	Caernarvonshire, nr Betws-y-Coed	13th cent (Welsh built)	rectangular great tower
31	Donnington	Berkshire, nr Newbury	14th cent	rectangular plan
32	Dover	Kent	11th–14th cents	concentric, with rectangul great tower
33	Dunstaffnage	Argyllshire, on Loch Etive	13th cent	curtain and towers
34	Dunstanburgh	Northumberland, nr Alnwick	14th–15th cents	curtain and flanking towe
35	Ewloe	Flintshire, nr Hawarden	13th cent (Welsh built)	round towers
36	Farnham	Surrey	12th–13th cents	motte-and-bailey, shell wi rectangular tower
37	Flint	Flintshire	13th cent	quadrangle of towers on corners
38	Framlingham	Suffolk	end 12th cent	curtain and flanking towe
39	Goodrich	Herefordshire, nr Ross-on-Wye	12th, 13th, 14th cents	rectangular great tower in concentric plan of later da

Unusual features	*Whether besieged, and if so, when*	*Historical associations*
	1544	murder of Darnley planned here
gatehouse round extension	1404, 1450	
possibly unique in Europe; arly 150 embrasures for ing	Civil War	
gular gatehouse with three wers		
gatehouse	1298, 1650	featured in Gowrie Conspiracy
in had two square towers	1282	used as quarry for materials for Caernarvon
	1283	birthplace (probably) of Llywelyn the Great
gatehouse, much naining	Civil War	held out against Parliament for nearly two years, 1644–6
Constable's Gate; some lls 20ft thick	1216, Civil War	outer defences mined, 1216
		Flora MacDonald imprisoned for a while, 1746
twin-round-tower tehouse	Wars of Roses	owned by John of Gaunt who made gatehouse into a keep
		built by Welsh to threaten Chester
	1216, Civil War	
ower much larger than ner three		
ing towers square	1215	refuge of Mary Tudor, 1553, when Duke of Northumberland tried to make Lady Jane Grey queen
barbican	1326, Civil War	

	Castle	County and nearest town	Principal centuries of construction	Type of castle
40	Harlech	Merionethshire	13th cent	concentric
41	Hedingham	Essex, nr Halstead	12th cent	early rectangular great tow
42	Helmsley	Yorkshire, nr Thirsk	13th cent	rectangular great tower, curtain and towers
43	Hermitage	Roxburghshire	14th–15th cents	rectangular tower-house
44	Kenilworth	Warwickshire	12th–14th cents	rectangular great tower, curtain
45	Kidwelly	Carmarthenshire	13th–15th cents	quadrangle of round towe outer curtain of towers, tw gatehouses
46	Kildrummie	Aberdeenshire	13th cent	rectangular bailey with co towers
47	Launceston	Cornwall	11th, 14th cents	motte-and-bailey, shell ke gatehouse
48	Llanstephan	Carmarthenshire	11th–13th cents	curtain with towers
49	Middleham	Yorkshire	12th–13th cents	rectangular great tower
50	Norham	Northumberland, nr Berwick	12th–15th cents	early great tower, oval cur
51	Nunney	Somerset, Frome	14th cent	tower, with more towers angles
52	Ogmore	Glamorganshire	12th–14th cents	rectangular great tower
53	Orford	Suffolk	12th cent	polygonal great tower, wit buttresses
54	Pendennis	Cornwall, Falmouth	16th cent	many-sided wall with cent circular tower
55	Pevensey	Sussex	11th–13th cents (and of course Roman)	tower and curtain
56	Peveril	Derbyshire	11th–13th cents	rectangular great tower
57	Pontefract	Yorkshire	11th–13th cents	shell keep of trefoil plan

Unusual features	*Whether besieged, and if so, when*	*Historical associations*
gatehouse	1294, 1403, 1468, Civil War	HQ of Owain Glyndŵr, beginning of 15th cent
as crosswall in great hall	1216	home of de Veres for centuries
	Civil War	
archway		home of Bothwell family
of Gaunt's Great Hall	1266, Civil War	belonged to Simon de Montfort and later to John of Gaunt
st concentric	1215	
entric appearance		George Fox, first Quaker, imprisoned 1656
gatehouse	1146, 1215	owned for a while by boy Edward V
		favourite home of Richard III
tower has crosswall	1215, 1318, 1322, 1327, 1463, 1497, 1513	border fortress
ied residence of French ign	1645	surrendered in Civil War very swiftly
ty-one faces; circular inner e	1216	built by Henry II to contain Bigod, Earl of Norfolk
	1646	
part of Roman wall and ts	1088, 1147, 1240, 1264	
barbicans		scene of alleged murder of Richard II

	Castle	*County and nearest town*	*Principal centuries of construction*	*Type of castle*
58	Portchester	Hampshire, Portsmouth	11th–12th cents (and of course Roman)	rectangular great tower in part Roman curtain
59	Raglan	Monmouthshire	15th–16th cents	hexagonal great tower
60	Restormel	Cornwall	12th–13th cents	motte, shell keep, with ga
61	Rhuddlan	Flintshire	11th–13th cents	motte, with later concentr quadrangle
62	Richmond	Yorkshire	11th–13th cents	rectangular great tower at apex of triangular curtain bailey
63	Rochester	Kent	12th–13th cents	rectangular great tower a curtain
64	Rothesay	Bute	13th cent	shell keep and towers, insi a moat
65	St Mawes	Cornwall	16th cent	round towered fort for co defence
66	Scarborough	Yorkshire	12th–14th cents	rectangular great tower
67	Skenfrith	Monmouthshire, nr Abergavenny	13th cent	round great tower, quad-rangular curtain and tow
68	Sween	Argyllshire	13th cent	rectangular great tower o Norman design
69	Tantallon	East Lothian	14th–15th cents	rectangular curtain and to on promontory
70	Tattershall	Lincolnshire	15th cent	quadrangle with moat, towers and big gatehouse
71	Threave	Kirkcudbright-shire	14th cent	rectangular tower-house, curtain with towers
72	Totnes	Devonshire	early 12th cent	shell keep on old motte rebuilt 14th cent
73	Tower of London		11th–20th cents	rectangular great tower o 11th cent inside concentri plan curtains and towers
74	Tretower	Brecknockshire	12th–13th cents	round great tower inside polygonal curtain

Unusual features	*Whether besieged, and if so, when*	*Historical associations*
er sited in one corner of uadrangle		royal castle to 1632; used sometimes after that for foreign captives
er adjacent to other uildings. Good examples of achicolation	Civil War	
	1644	
large gatehouses	Civil War	statute of Rhuddlan issued here
		royal castle for centuries
corner mined in 1216, faced with round turret	1216, 1264	
of very few Scottish shell eeps	1230	probably besieged and taken by Vikings
oil plan	Civil War	
er over 100ft at one time	1312, 1536, 1645	besieged by army of Pilgrimage of Grace, 1536
		built and owned by Hubert de Burgh
ibly oldest great tower in cotland	1645	built when this part of Argyll was in Viking hands
	1491, 1528	captured by Cromwell, 1651
ely built of red brick		
-storeyed	1455, 1545, Civil War	owned by Black Douglas family
nded end to one corner of ower; unique strategic osition	1381 (during Peasants' Revolt)	legion

	Castle	*County and nearest town*	*Principal centuries of construction*	*Type of castle*
75	Warkworth	Northumberland	13th–14th cents	quadrangle with great to at one end
76	Warwick	Warwickshire	14th cent	curtain and towers, some tall
77	Windsor	Berkshire	11th–15th cents	motte and two baileys wi additions such as shell kee curtain, towers, etc

Unusual features	*Whether besieged, and if so, when*	*Historical associations*
wer rectangular with cut corners; tall look-out tower at top	1405	figured in Percy revolt against Henry IV
ge gatehouse, fine barbican, most of structure restored		Used by Richard Nevill, Earl of Warwick (the Kingmaker)
		residence of royal family for generations

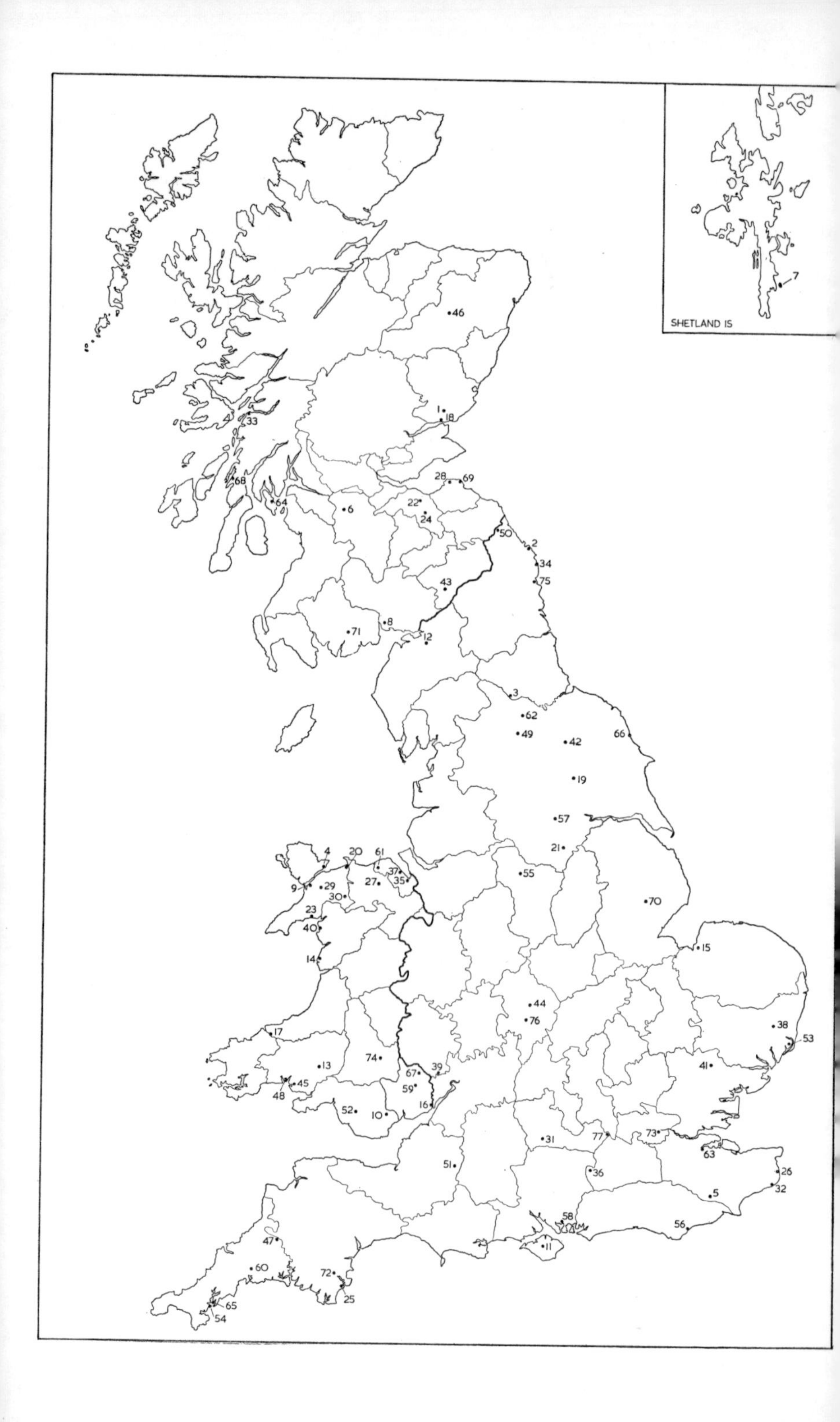

SHETLAND IS
7
46
1
18
33
68
64
28
69
22
24
6
50
2
34
75
43
8
71
12
3
62
49
42
66
19
57
21
4
20
61
37
35
9
29
27
30
55
70
23
40
14
15
44
76
17
38
53
13
74
67
39
59
48
45
41
52
10
16
73
77
31
63
51
36
26
32
5
58
56
11
47
60
72
25
65
54

GLOSSARY OF TERMS

Apse	circular or polygonal end of a chapel or aisle, hence apsidal tower, a D-end to a corner tower
Arbalest	a type of powerful crossbow with a mechanical device for bending the bow and a trigger to release the string and discharge the dart
Ashlar	squared blocks of smooth stone, the best said to have come from Caen in Normandy
Bailey	courtyard or ward, that is, area inside walls of castle or of palisade
Ballista	siege engine in the shape of a large bow for firing stones
Barbican	outward continuation of a gateway, to defend it, often in the form of a walled passage without a roof
Bartizan	small tower or turret projecting from a larger tower or from battlements
Bastion	another word for a corner tower of a quadrangle, or a flanking tower with an open rear
Battering Wall	the splayed part of the base of a curtain
Berm	the horizontal space between a curtain or tower and the moat
Belfry	tall wooden tower on wheels, used in siege operations
Buttress	projecting pillar on wall added to strengthen it
Chevron moulding	moulding in the form of chevrons, that is, in inverted 'V's, a feature of Norman architectural decoration
Corbel	a stone bracket projecting from a wall

Crenellation openings in the upper part of a parapet; the projecting vertical parts were merlons and the spaces embrasures

Curtain general term for a castle wall, whether inner, outer or part of a quadrangle keep (like Tantallon)

Donjon another word for great tower, but not often used. Bothwell is one well-known castle where the great tower is usually called the donjon

Drawbridge a wooden bridge which could be lifted to prevent access across a moat into a gatehouse or gateway

Drum Tower round tower built into a wall, such as at Flint Castle

Forebuilding a structure on the outside wall of a great tower protecting the entry door, and all, or part, of the approaching stairway. Usually these were a storey or two less in height than the tower, but at Castle Rising the forebuilding is of the same height

Garderobe correct term for lavatory or latrine in a castle

Glacis smooth, gentle slope, especially an external slope of a castle without cover from weapon fire

Great Tower correct word for rectangular, polygonal or round main building associated with Norman castles, usually but incorrectly called keep (see Donjon)

Gun-loop an opening in the wall for a gun barrel. Gun-loops are particularly noticeable at Claypotts, Angus

Hoarding a covered wooden gallery affixed to the top of the outside of a tower or curtain, to defend the castle. It was supported on wooden beams inserted into put-log holes. The floor was partly slatted to allow dropping of missiles on besiegers. This led to the development of machicolation

MACHICOLATION	a projecting part of a parapet with holes in the floor through which missiles or liquids were dropped on besiegers. Machicolation was in stonework, and was sometimes added to existing buildings, as at Caerlaverock
MANGONEL	a stone-throwing machine
MANTLET	a mobile wooden shield on wheels for archers to hide behind when attacking defenders on the ramparts
MOTTE	mound of earth, either natural or thrown up by diggers, on which a wooden (or, later, a stone) tower was built
MURDER-HOLE	an opening in the roof of a gateway through which missiles were dropped on successful besiegers
ORIEL WINDOWS	projecting windows in an upper storey, more usually called bay windows today
OUBLIETTE	a dungeon under the floor of a room, reached by a trap-door, or more loosely, a passage leading from upper rooms to a moat for disposal of drainage or unwanted or troublesome persons
PENTHOUSE	a square-section mobile tunnel made by a besieging army and run up close to a castle's wall to protect men beneath charging the wall with a battering ram
PHAROS	a lighthouse or beacon to guide navigators
PORTCULLIS	wood and iron grille-pattern gate which was raised and lowered in grooves by ropes or chains in or in front of a gateway
POSTERN	small gateway, usually in the side flanks of a castle
PUT-LOG	beam inserted into special holes in a great tower at wall-walk level to support hoarding in case of attack
REVET	to face with a layer of stone, stone slabs, etc for increased strength and support
SHELL KEEP	a castle in the form of a circular or oval or

polygonal walled enclosure on a mound (Restormel, Carisbrooke, etc). The shell might be part of a larger whole inside a curtain

SLIGHTING — deliberately damaging a castle to render it unfit for occupation or for use as a fortress. This was often done by blowing up parts of towers or walls by gunpowder or in earlier times, perhaps, using Greek Fire

SLIT — a thin aperture in a wall through which arrows could be fired with some protection against retaliation. Unfortunately, the usual way in which these were built prevented the archers from seeing anywhere other than forwards. As apertures for light, they were inadequate

SOLAR — the private quarters of a lord, sometimes adjacent to the dining hall, sometimes on a different storey, in a great tower

TREBUCHET — a siege engine in the shape of a huge sling

WARD — bailey or courtyard

REFERENCES AND READING LIST

The list of books and journals below represents some of the great quantity of matter studied in the production of this sketch of British castles. In addition, the Department of the Environment, which in 1970 absorbed the Ministry of Public Building and Works in whose care the great majority of the best British castles reposed, produces official guides to more than 100 major medieval castles. These are essential reading for anyone who wants to know more about British castles. They are listed in the booklet *Ancient Monuments and Historic Buildings*, obtainable free from HMSO bookshops or at selected booksellers throughout the UK.

Anglo-Saxon Chronicle, trans G. N. Garmonsway (1953)
Archaeologia Cambrensis, various issues
Armitage, E. S. *Early Norman Castles* (1912)
Arnold, Ralph. *Social History of England* (1967)
Ashdown, Charles. *British Castles* (1911)
Bagley, J. J. *Life in Mediaeval England* (1960)
Brown, R. Allen. *English Mediaeval Castles* (1954)
Bryant, Sir Arthur. *The Age of Chivalry* (1963)
Cambridge Mediaeval History, various volumes
Castles of Wales (1971)
Coulton, G. G. *Mediaeval Panorama* (1938)
Cruden, Stewart. *The Scottish Castle* (1963)
Davis, R. H. C. *King Stephen* (1967)
Dictionary of National Biography
Earnshaw, Walter. *Discovering Castles* (1953)
Ellis, P. B. *Wales, a Nation Again!* (1968)
Erskine, S. R. J. *Macbeth, King of Scotland* (1930)

Harvey, A. *The Castles and Walled Towns of England* (1925)
History of the King's Works, The, HMSO (1963)
Hollister, C. W. *The Military Organization of Norman England* (1965)
Larousse, Encyclopaedia of Ancient and Mediaeval History (1967)
Lloyd, Sir John. *History of Wales from the Earliest Times to the Edwardian Conquest*, two volumes (1939)
MacKenzie, W. M. *The Mediaeval Castle in Scotland* (1927)
Myers, A. R. *England in the Late Middle Ages (1307–1536)* (1956)
O'Neil, B. H. St J. *Castles* (1953)
Painter, S. *The Reign of King John* (1949)
Poole, A. L. *From Domesday to Magna Carta* (1955)
——. *Mediaeval England* (1958)
Powicke, Sir Maurice. *Henry III and the Lord Edward* (1952)
Quennell, Marjorie and C. H. B. *History of Everyday Things in England, 1066–1799* (1931)
Renn, D. *Norman Castles in Britain* (1968)
Stenning, E. H. *The Isle of Man* (1950)
Thompson, A. H. *Military Architecture in England during the Middle Ages* (1912)
Tomkieff, O. G. *Life in Norman England* (1958)
Tout, T. F. *Edward the First* (1902)
——. *Political History of England* (1898)
Trevelyan, G. M. *English Social History* (1946)
Wheeler, Sir Mortimer. *Segontium and the Roman Occupation of Wales* (1924)
Whitelock, Douglas. *The Norman Conquest: its setting and impact* (1966)
Wilkinson, B. *The Later Middle Ages in England* (1969)
Williams, T. D. *The Last Welsh Prince, Llywelyn ap Gruffydd* (1970)
Wood, C. T. *The Age of Chivalry* (1970)

INDEX